Forex Trading Fc
The Ultimate Strategies On How To Profit In Trading And Generate Passive Income

Also by Leonardo Turner

Real Estate Investing Blueprint For Beginners How To Create Passive Income On Properties To Escape The Rat Race And Reach Financial freedom
Stock Market Investing For Beginners Learn Strategies To Profit In Stock Trading, Day Trading And Generate Passive Income
Stock Market Investing + Real Estate Investing For Beginners 2 Books in 1 Learn The Best Strategies To Generate Passive Income Day Trading, Investing In Stocks, And Investing In Real Estate
Forex Trading For Beginners The Ultimate Strategies On How To Profit In Trading And Generate Passive Income

1

Introduction

In this book, you will learn all the basic information you need to start understanding foreign exchange currencies, and how to trade them. You will learn exactly what Forex is, and why you should dabble in the art of trading it.

You will learn about the risk vs. the reward, and much much more. All lined out with clear and concise instructions, tips, and other indicators to make this book simple and enjoyable to read.

I hope you find what you need, and that this book is what gives you the push to start this fun adventure in the currency trading world.

Chapter 1: Forex Trading

Forex trading uses currency as the trading vehicle. Forex is short for foreign exchange, also known as FX and currency trading. It is an investment market, where you trade money, known as currency, where you do not trade USD for USD, but USD for Euros, Yen, Australian dollars, and numerous other currencies used in countries around the world.

You make money trading in the forex market by determining which currency in a pair will move up or down in value faster or in the opposite direction from the other currency in the pair.

EUR/USD is the euro and US dollar currency pair. The EUR is called the base currency, and it is always equal to 1. The USD is the quote currency and it will change in value against the EUR. If you see 1 EUR/USD= 1.11967, it is read as for 1 euro you will receive 1.11967 US dollars in an over the counter trade.

If you walked into a bank and asked for 100 euros to be exchanged into USD, you would be given $111.99 dollars. If you walked into that same bank and said you need to exchange $100 USD for euros, you would be given 89.29 euros based on the exchange rate mentioned above.

This type of currency exchange is common and what travelers do each year, but it is not how investors make money in forex trading. The money is actually made based on the bid and ask price or the buy and sell price of a currency pair, and whether the currency pair is going to gain or lose in value.

Image 1: Bid/Ask Chart
EUR/USD Time Stamp (in GMT)
1.11967 Sell 1.11962 Buy

The chart shows you the most typical way information is presented. You will see what currency pair the quote information is about and the time the quote is being provided. There are also boxes that show the low and high for the day, before giving you the sell and buy or ask and bid price for the currency. Some charts just offer the currency pair and the bid/ask price.

It is your job as a trader to determine if you want to sell euros and buy USD because the USD will become stronger or if you want to buy euro and sell USD because the USD will become weaker, against the EUR.

The point that many traders become confused on is what strong or weak means in a currency pair. The easiest way to define this is to look at how far your base currency goes in an exchange.

In the EUR/USD pair, you can use fewer EUR to gain more USD. However, you need more USD to gain fewer euros. Now, let's look at the exchange above again. You gained 111.99 USD for 100 euros, but only 89.29 euros for 100 USD.

So, let's now answer the question of what has more value. You traded less euros to get more USD. You traded more USD to get fewer euros. In this equation your euros hold more value against the USD because the euro goes further when traded in for USD. When you travel, you want your domestic currency to hold more value, so you spend less of it. When you come back from your travels, you want your international currency to provide you with more of your domestic currency.

If you think in those terms, then it will be easier to understand why value is so important to the forex market and retail traders. You are considered a retail trader, but you are also not the only player in the market.

You can also remember these little hints:

1. The base currency is stronger than the quote currency equals a rising currency pair. (The price will be rising on a chart)

2. The base currency is weaker than the quote currency equals a falling currency pair. (The price will be falling on a chart)

3. The quote currency is weaker than the base currency equals a rising currency pair. (The price will be in an upward trend on the chart) *

4. The quote currency is stronger than the base currency equals a falling currency pair. (The price will be in a downward trend on the chart) *

*Upward and downward trends will be explained in technical analysis.

Why Do Currency Prices Change?

Understanding why currency prices change comes down to predicting how they are going to move under certain conditions. Once you, as a currency trader, are able to predict currency movements you are able to invest for a profit.

When you learn about strategies like fundamental analysis you are going to be able to answer the following:

• What drives currency prices? The simple answer is supply and demand, but it requires a more in depth discussion to fully grasp currency movement.

• Who drives the currency prices? You, big banks, corporations, governments, and the interbank system are largely responsible for currency price movements. Each has a cog to play in the wheel of forex.

• What are the individual personalities of the currencies? All currencies have their own general forces that drive them to move, which can vary due to economic situations and government involvement.

• How will currencies react to economic reports/announcements and news? Economic reports can change a pattern in currency movements depending on what they are, when they happen, and the scale of the news.

• Which indicators do you need to watch to succeed? Indicators are early warning signs that the market is going to change and you can begin to predict currency movement by watching proper indicators.

How Do You Profit from that Movement?

Once you have a grasp on why currencies move, you can develop strategies that help you profit from those movements. You will learn the following as you gain more understanding of forex trading:

- Where you invest your money—spot, ETF, futures, etc.
- How to execute short-term trades.
- How to invest for long-term.
- How to protect your investment.

Chapter 2: How To Choose Currencies To Trade

Forex trading is about currencies. Choosing the right currency pair to trade in is the first and foremost decision that you have to make in a forex transaction.

Factors to consider

1. Market
2. Timing
3. Currency pair type
4. Correlations

Market

As we have discussed before, there are several forex markets. These markets are based on:

• Geographic location – By geographic location, we do have New York market, London market, Hong Kong market, Singapore market, etc.

• Nature of transaction – By nature of the transaction, we do have spot market, day market, forwards market, futures market, etc.

Ultimately, you will need to use both geographic location and nature of the transaction to narrow down to your particular market e.g. London Futures, etc.

Timing

You have to know the right moment for trading in your market. Then, you can be able to anticipate the most optimal currency pair to trade in during that time. This is because time influences the performance of each currency pair in a particular market.

Currency Pair Type

As we discussed previously, the following are the currency pair types

• Majors

- Crosses
- Exotics

Majors

The following are the list of Major currencies and their respective geographic markets.

Globally:

- EUR/USD – "Euro"
- USD/JPY – "Gopher"
- GBP/USD – "Cable"
- AUD/USD – "Aussie"
- USD/CHF – "Swissie"
- USD/CAD – "Loonie"

London:

- EUR/USD
- GBP/USD
- USD/JPY
- AUD/USD
- USD/CHF
- USD/CAD

New York:

- EUR/USD
- USD/JPY
- GBP/USD
- AUD/USD
- USD/CAD
- USD/CHF

Tokyo:

- USD/JPY
- EUR/USD
- AUD/USD
- GBP/USD

Australia:

- AUD/USD
- EUR/USD
- USD/JPY
- GBP/USD
- USD/CAD
- USD/CHF

Singapore

- EUR/USD
- USD/JPY
- GBP/USD
- AUD/USD
- USD/CAD
- USD/CHF

Crosses

The following are the most popular crosses and their respective markets

Globally:

- EUR/JPY – Euro vs. Japanese Yen
- EUR/GBP – Euro vs. British Pound
- EUR/NZD – Euro vs. the New Zealand dollar
- EUR/AUD – Euro vs. the Australian dollar
- GBP/JPY – British pound vs. the Japanese yen
- AUD/CAD – Australian dollar vs. the Canadian dollar
- EUR/GBP – Euro vs. the British pound
- AUD/NZD – Aussie dollar vs. the New Zealand dollar
- GBP/AUD – British pound vs. the Australian dollar
- AUD/JPY – Australian dollar vs. the Japanese yen
- NZD/JPY – New Zealand dollar vs. the Japanese yen
- AUD/CHF – Australian dollar vs. the Swiss franc
- EUR/CHF – Euro vs. the Swiss franc
- CHF/JPY – Swiss franc vs. the Japanese yen
- EUR/JPY – Euro vs. the Japanese yen

- EUR/CAD – Euro vs. the Canadian dollar
- GBP/CHF – British pound vs. the Swiss franc
- CAD/JPY – Canadian dollar vs. the Japanese yen

London:
- EUR/GBP
- EUR/JPY

New York:
- EUR/JPY
- EUR/CHF
- EUR/GBP

Tokyo:
- EUR/JPY

Australia:
- EUR/JPY
- EUR/GBP

Singapore:
- EUR/JPY

Exotics:

The most popular exotics are:
- USD/TRY – U.S. dollar vs. the Turkish lira
- USD/MXN – U.S. dollar vs. the Mexican peso
- USD/ZAR – U.S. dollar vs. the South African Rand
- EUR/TRY – Euro vs. the Turkish lira
- USD/BRL – U.S. dollar vs. the Brazilian real

Correlations

Most major currency pairs are correlated in their price movement. For example, the EUR/USD and the GBP/USD tend to move in the same general direction, though the GPB/USD is relatively more volatile than the EUR/USD. This shows positive correlation. Thus, if either of the two currencies is up, you can assume the other one too to be up, and vice versa.

The USD/CHF and EUR/USD tend to move in the opposite direction. This shows they are negatively correlated. Thus, if either of the two currencies is up, you can assume the other one to be down, and vice versa.

If you enter a long on two currency pairs that are positively correlated, you are simply doubling your risk. Similarly, if you enter a long position one pair and a short on another pair of two pairs that are negatively correlated, you are still doubling your risk.

Steps to following in selecting the best currency pairs

1. Test at least 8 currency pairs on a chart – This will help you determine pairs on uptrend, consolidating pairs, and pairs under pressure. You can also be able to determine if there is a certain currency going against the general trade.

2. Scan through latest market reports – Through scanning, you gauge latest market sentiments and the risk-on/risk-off situation of the most likely currency pair to transact. Naturally, you would seek to avoid those currencies exhibiting high volatility risk.

3. Pair the stronger against the weaker currencies - Best currency pair to trade is the trending one. A pair exhibiting strong trend is usually pushed by a strong base currency and aided by a weaker counter-currency. For example, the GBP/USD pair will be on a strong uptrend if the GBP is strengthening while the USD is weakening. On the other hand, the USD/JPY will move in a strong downtrend if the USD is weakening and the JPY is strengthening. Also pairing a currency with higher volatility against a currency that has been consolidating can make a trick.

4. Carry out Technical Analysis – Make a quick technical chart analysis on your preferred pairs to establish trends and ranges. This helps you narrow down to the best currency pairs, which are in line with the strongest trends. Make incisive analysis to identify the resistance, support, and pivot levels. Check your open positions to confirm if your preferred currencies are included. This is important for

diversification. If you are already in an EUR/USD, for diversification purposes, it is good to exclude a currency pair that has the Euro.

5. Shortlist your currency pairs – Your choice will depend on recent global risk events, your portfolio, and your trading personality (risk averse or risk taker). If you are a risk taker with ample time to follow-up on market performances, then, going for currencies represented by economies with potential event risk could work for you. On the other hand, if you are risk-averse, and probably you may not have time to follow-up on market performances, then go for a currency representing a stable economic future. Do the same for both majors and crosses to diversify your portfolio.

6. Compute the pip value and accompanying risks – It follows that some currency pairs have a high pip value compared to others. While higher pip value can increase your profitability in winnings, it can also increase your losses in the opposite direction. Thus, you need to compute your tolerance limits and adjust your limit and stop order levels appropriately. This will grant you the confidence that even if a risk occurs, you will not lose more than you can withstand.

7. Move against the crowd – Try to trade against the majority of the crowds. The crowds have the power to push or pull in a certain direction thus nullifying the intended outcome. Going against the crowd can help you reap the spillover benefits. Following up on market sentiments, more so from news and social media can help you reveal such sentiments. Scutify is a social media dedicated to financial events. It can help you get a feel of the prevailing market sentiments.

Currency watch list

A currency watch list is important in helping you establish a currency pair that is best performing at a given time to optimize your earnings. Check on your trading platform on how to set up a watch list. Meta4Trader has a way by which you can set up an automated watch list.

Chapter 3: Advantages and Disadvantages Of Forex Trading

Forex trading has its advantages and disadvantages. It is important that you know about them, so that you will know what to expect once you start trading foreign currencies. Let us examine them one by one:

Advantages

• High-profit potential

Forex trading has a high-profit potential. In fact, there are professional FX traders who have quit their day job and trade currencies for a living. Some people have also attained financial freedom by forex trading. Trading currencies has long been established as something that can be very lucrative. Of course, you also need to spend time and efforts in order to make it worthwhile and profitable. When you engage in FX trading, even a small investment of $100 can grow by more than 300% in just a short period of time. Compare this with investing in stocks where a profit of 20% in a year is already considered high. Indeed, if you have money that you can use to invest, learning forex trading is most probably the best thing that you can do that can lead you to financial freedom.

• Leverage

It is not a secret that many people like forex trading because it will allow you to leverage.

Needless to say, this will allow you to rake in more profits. Many traders do not have enough money to start up with a decent capital. Leveraging will allow you to spend and risk less and at the same time have a high-profit return.

• Low cost

The main cost in forex trading is normally included already in the spread. Therefore, you no longer need to worry about any exchange or clearing fee, and not even a brokerage fee. Under normal market conditions, the retail transaction cost is even lower than 0.1%. If you are working with a large dealer, then it is normally lower than 0.7%. Of course, this may increase depending on your leverage. Since you no longer have to worry about so many costs that you need to cover, you can put all your focus on what really matters, and that is making a profit.

• High liquidity

The FX market is famous for having high liquidity. Therefore, you can expect to be able to buy and sell currencies easily since there is always someone who will take the other side of your trade. You can never get "stuck" and there is definitely no waiting time for buying and selling currencies. It is a very active market.

• 24-hour market

The forex market is open round-the-clock. Hence, you can trade in the morning, in the afternoon, in the evening, or evening at 2am or 3am. It is up to you to decide when you want to participate in the market. Although the forex market follows a schedule, once it opens for the week, you can rest assured that it will remain open round the clock until it closes by the end of the week.

• Fair market

There is no authority that controls or unduly influences the forex market. Of course, certain things and event may affect the price of currencies, but they cannot continuously do so for an extended period of time. The forex market is very big with lots of different participants.

• Easy to enter

It is easy to enter the forex market. You can start participating in the market simply by going online. You can make trades in the comfort of your home. You also do not need a high capital. There are many online brokers that will allow you to trade even with a small investment.

- Convenient

Forex trading is convenient to do. All you need is to connect to the Internet and you can start trading using the trading platform that is provided by your broker. You can easily open and close positions with just a few clicks of a mouse.

- More choices

With around 28 major currency pairs to choose from, you will never run out of currency pairs to trade. This ensures that you will not find a moment to sit idly. Also, considering the nature of forex, you are sure that there is always a currency pair among the chances that will make profits.

- Demo account

Most forex traders will allow you to preview their services by providing you with a demo account. A demo account will allow you not only to test your broker's trading platform, but it will also allow you to trade in a real-market environment. A demo account can also be used to test your strategy. As a forex broker, testing your strategy before using it with real money is an important habit that you definitely have to do.

- Fun

Trading currencies is fun to do. In fact, it is very easy to get addicted to it. It is like a game that adults can truly enjoy, especially if you are making positive profits. It is fun to look at charts and choose the currency pair that you want to invest in. Developing a strategy and making your own market predictions can be fun. Overall, the whole activity of being a forex trader can be a truly fun experience.

Disadvantages

- Risky

Although people who engage in forex trading are in it for the profit that they can make, the unfortunate truth is that many of these traders end up losing their investment. It is risky to participate in forex, especially if you do not know what you are doing. In fact, if you do not have knowledge of forex and simply jump in without preparation, it is most likely that you will suffer a big loss in just a few days. If you get too careless, then you can expect to lose your money on the very first day of trading. Even those who have been trading for years are still careful before they open a position. As a beginner, you need to be more cautious of your actions.

Although you are well encouraged to do all the necessary research and analysis before making any trade, there is no amount of preparation that can guarantee 100% it will give you a favorable outcome. Literally every trade that you make has its risks.

• Lower return

It is true that you can make lots of money with forex even if you just invest a small amount since you can use the power leverage. It is also true that trading currencies has a higher profit potential than just investing in stocks. However, forex trading is not the one that offers the highest payout. Of you want a higher return, then you might want to consider options trading instead of forex trading. With options trading, you can get as high as 90% return for every trade that lasts as fast as two minutes, or even less. However, it is worth noting that options trading is so much riskier than forex trading. Options trading is like gambling in the casino. There is also no way to leverage your position.

• Volatility

The prices of different currencies are affected by many factors. The forex market can, from time to time, be highly volatile. You can also expect for some unforeseeable events to take place. The bad part is that traders may not be able to do anything about them when they occur. For example, during the time when Iceland got bankrupt, forex traders holding Icelandic krona could not do anything but watch how they were holding a something that has significantly depreciated. This is unlike in investing in stocks where shareholders can somehow pressure the board of directors to act more promptly and take appropriate actions. To avoid being a victim of the high volatility of the market, it is well advised that you limit your losses and always be sure to use a well-planned approach when trading.

• Less regulated

Since forex trading is not regulated by any central authority, traders usually rely on their broker to facilitate a trade. If you get lucky and end up working with an unreliable broker, you will only get scammed and cheated in the process. Also, since you will be relying on the assistance extended to you by a broker, you may not have total control over your trades and orders. Therefore, in order to prevent this from happening, it is important that you only work with regulated and legitimate brokers. Since forex takes place in an over-the-counter market, you need to be careful in choosing your broker.

• Self-taught

Unlike investing in stocks where you can ask for assistance from trade advisors and portfolio managers, dealing with forex is ultimately something that you do on your own. It is not a surprise for beginners to lose their initial investment. Unfortunately, after experiencing a bad loss, they usually get discouraged, which prevents them from fully learning the ins and outs of trading. Hence, when you are just starting out, it is important that you admit to yourself that you are just a newbie. As much as possible, take advantage of the demo account that is provided to you by your broker, so that you can familiarize yourself with the actual trading environment. It is also advised that you start out small even if you have a big amount of money that ready for trading in your account.

• Hard to predict

There are multiple factors that affect the forex market. In fact, this is the reason why forex traders usually rely on technical analysis. With so many factors that influence the prices of the different currencies, it becomes almost impossible to predict the price movement of a currency. Of course, you can always apply an effective strategy, but it does not change the fact that the forex market is hard, if not impossible, to predict.

If you were to consider all the elements that can influence the outcome of a particular trade, then you will have to spend lots of hours just to be able to analyze everything. However, the forex market is a continuously moving market. Therefore, by the time that you finish analyzing a set of data, there will definitely be a new set of information that you could look into.

Chapter 4: Trading Styles And Strategies

Trading styles

Success in Forex trading is dependent on your trading style and strategies that you choose to engage in. As a beginner trader, you will want to find the ideal trading style to suit you.

The time frame involved in the different trading styles is a key factor in determining the best style for you. Trading styles can offer short term trade positions (scalping) to medium term (example swing trade) to long-term (trend trading) situated on the farthest end of the time frame spectrum. Consider the demands on your time as a factor when choosing a trading style.

• Long-term time-frames

Long-term position traders sit are in it, as the name suggests, for the long run – months, sometimes year-long duration in the case of extended trend strategies. Traders choosing this time-frame want to take advantage of the prospective of reaping large profit margins. The assumption is that if you properly implement a trend style you stand a better chance of greater earning potential than you would gain in a shorter period.

One advantage of long-term trading is the relatively less focus required to monitor markets. This feature is countered by the level of patience traders require to remain invested in a trade.

• Medium-term time-frame

Medium-term trading offers a balance in trade time demands. Trade positions can remain open for a few days to sometimes a few weeks.

• Short-term time-frame

Scalpers practice short-term trading. Trades are open for a very short space of time – typically within a day – with only minor movements in price change needed. Because multiple trades need to be made in order to turn a profit, traders have to have the time and focus to take advantage here.

There are four common trading styles. These are scalping, day trading (also known as intraday trading), swing trading, and or trend trading (also referred to as longer term position trading). The style you settle on would depend on the type of person you are and what your lifestyle permits. A general overview of the trading style, its principles and benefits, is presented below.

Day trading for beginners

Day trading is the buying and selling of foreign currencies on the same day. It can even involve opening trades multiple times during the span of a day. One of the reasons traders choose day trading is so that they can take advantage of small price movements in the market. While this style can prove to be a profitable style if performed properly, it can also prove risky.

The principles involved in day trading:

• Keep up-to-date on market conditions

• It is essential that day traders do their homework and are continually updated on news and events that affect the currency exchange market.

• Know the amount of money you are willing to lose by setting a risk margin. As a beginner, you will want to risk the smallest margin on your trades.

• Have no limitations on your time

In order to be a successful day trader, you need to have time available to study the market, explore opportunities and respond promptly to market movements or broker re-quotes. These can happen at any time during open sessions.

Why would you choose Day trading?

The advantages of this trading style include:

• Make as many trades as you want

You can open and close as many trade positions as you want. The potential to make money quickly (dependent on favorable market factors) is possible.

- The overnight risk is removed

One of the challenges of holding a trade position open overnight is that there is a higher risk of your trade being affected by dramatic market developments while you are asleep and when you are not able to take the relevant decisions. You have peace of mind.

- Maximize leverage

Day traders generally make the most of leverage ratios they are offered and with the benefit a low margin. The opportunity of increasing profit is maximized.

- Accelerates trading knowledge and experience

Day traders gain more experience trading faster in relation to other trading styles as they can open and close more trade positions based on their study of the market conditions.

Day trading does require time, discipline and commitment in order to be a profit-making trading style.

Scalping for beginners

Scalping is recognized as a specialized trading style that offers opportunities to make small gains based on small market price changes usually soon once a trade is entered into and shows profitability. The idea here is to make money by securing more wins in a longer time-frame. Another belief is that the forex market experiences smaller movements more frequently even during quiet times.

The principles involved in scalping

- Quick exit strategy required

As profits made are small, the potential to lose any gains made in the event of a substantial loss is considerable. One of the underlying expectations that apply to scalping is that the price movement of foreign exchange will move in the desired trend for a short duration, but thereafter the direction onwards remains uncertain – it can drop or rise.

• Many trade positions are required

As mentioned before, one feature of this trading style is that profits have a small margin; therefore, in order for a trader to make good money, he or she will need to engage in as many trades as possible.

• Discipline is essential

Scalping is a disciplined trading style that requires traders to make decisions quickly, constantly monitoring the market and have the patience to appreciate small profit margins of each trade.

Why would you choose scalping?

• Risk is limited

Keeping trade positions open for a brief period reduces exposure to risk. There is less chance of a trade being exposed to negative circumstances.

• Higher frequencies of trade provide greater earnings

Scalpers can quite easily engage in hundreds of trades over the course of a day with no one trade posing the risk of a big loss. This opens up the potential for big earnings when profits earned are compounded.

• There is always an opportunity for trade

While some styles are totally dependent on significant movement in the market, this is less so for scalpers. This is because the market is never stagnant; there will always be movement even if it is at a fraction, and that is all the movement that is needed for a scalper.

Scalping is a numbers game, not one dependent on the size of the trade.

Swing trading for beginners

Swing trading is a style suited to traders who can respond promptly to events that affect the market. Traders act quickly to profit from positive swings or if there is a downturn affecting their trade position, they are quick to initiate an exit strategy.

The principles involved in swing trading

• Market volatility required

Market volatility is an important prerequisite as increases in short-term price moves presents more opportunities to trade.

• Favors technical-based strategies

Technical traders work within specific parameters that help in their decision-making process of when to open/close trade positions, and risk is limited.

• Larger Stop-Loss orders required

The fact that swing trading holds trades open for more than one day, in order to limit risk, traders are encouraged to set up larger Stop-Loss orders.

Why would you choose swing trading?

• More trading opportunities

Seeing that the foreign exchange market is conditioned by a natural cycle (ebb and flow) regular trading opportunities abound. There is a constant change of rising and falling prices to cultivate a favorable environment to buy and sell.

• No need for additional deposit

Opening and closing positions in a matter of days allows you to identify opportunities for new positions to set up, requiring no deposit between the opening and closing trades.

Swing trading is particularly suited for novice traders as there are plenty of opportunities to trade and positions do not have to be opened for lengthy periods of time, increasing vulnerability to risk due to unforeseen events. Only a reasonable amount of time is required to monitor market activity.

Trend trading for beginners

Trend trading is regarded as one of the simpler styles to operate that offers effective and user-friendly methods to trade successfully. Trending is based on recognizing a trend, opening a trade and exiting once there is a reverse movement on the trend. Trades are held for the long term, a time-frame that allows for larger-than-average returns to be gained. This is the style to adopt if your goal is to reap large yields in profit.

The principles involved in trend trading

• Using tools to identify trends

Trend traders utilize a number of statistical tools and instruments to identify and benefit from Forex trading. Some of these instruments include charts, technical indicators and

• Designed to generate wealth

Trend trading offers the most risk-reducing approach to building wealth in the Forex market. Recognize a trend early, hold your position for a time and once you detect a reverse in the trend, exit quickly.

Why would you choose trend trading?

• Large profit margins without minute-by-minute market monitoring

This trading style doesn't require an intense focus on the market, yet the returns are greater than the norm.

• Fewer transaction costs

As a trend trader, you be engaged in fewer trades than a day trader. This means that with the fewer trade positions are less transaction costs that need to be paid.

Accurate analysis of market movement, discipline, determination and patience are strong requirements to reap the rewards of trend trading.

Trading strategies and approaches

You don't need complicated complex strategies to win at Forex trading. Sometimes the simpler strategies triumph over complex ones.

Find strategies you are comfortable with and that works for you and stick with those.

The next step is to choose a strategy that will allow you to make money from your trades at minimum risk to you. Once you have a strategy defined the next recommended advice is to practice, practice, practice before you invest any real money in it.

Various types of strategies

In Forex trading strategies are used to help traders make certain decisions like when to open a trade when to close a position as well as how to how to enter and exit a trade. Strategies can make use of a number of analytical and statistical tools and information-gathering methodologies. As the Forex market is a dynamic one, and with new innovations and developments in digital technology, trading strategies are updated to allow for improved analytical methods to support traders in their profit-making goals.

Fundamental analysis

The fundamental analysis strategy investigates the influence of major economic and political indicators that contribute to a currency's demand and supply, and which in return influences the currency exchange rate.

In dealing with economic indicators and other variables it is to be expected that this strategy is often experienced as tricky and complex to work with. Current news and data releases are some of the major sources of essential information.

Technical analysis

Technical analysis is another basic main artery of Foreign exchange trading strategies that are popular with many traders. This strategy is based on studying both past and the latest movements in currency prices. Information is plotted on charts which are then closely analyzed to ascertain onward movement. The reasoning behind this strategy is that market movement primarily decided by forces such as demand and supply that sets out the margins for increase or decrease in exchange rates. In using technical analysis, traders are provided with a scientific basis for engaging in a trade, making decision-making more concrete.

Range trading

This is a simple trading strategy that works on the principle that currency prices can maintain stability within a specified high and low range for a certain period of time. This holds true especially for currencies that are rarely manipulated by unforeseen events. The promise of predictability is a favorable factor here.

Momentum trading

Momentum trading is founded on the idea that the force of significant price movements along a specific course is a good indication that this price movement will likely proceed on this course. This strategy also takes into consideration that trends may weaken, indicating a reversal. Factors such as price and volume are critical here as is utilizing graphical instruments like candlestick charts.

An important note on trading strategies

As you have seen from the above there are a great many diverse approaches to trading in foreign currency. These work by understanding movements in price and how to profit from them. While you may find that relying on one specific strategy is simpler, no one strategy will be profitable all the time. It is suggested that you create your own hybrid version by using the complementary features of various strategies. As you are about to enter a market has is constantly changing, it is important for you to learn to adapt to these changes by having an array of resources available.

How to develop your own Forex trading strategy

At some point along your path, you may discover that you want to build your own trading strategy. What follows is a step-by-step guide to creating your own exclusive strategy to making money from currency trading.

Step 1: Decide on your time-frame

You first need to establish your trading style and the time-frame that best fits in with your goals and lifestyle. Do you have the time and are you willing to monitor the market and pore over technical data daily or weekly? How long are you willing to keep trade positions open? The time-frame you choose will determine the type of strategy you want to create. Don't be afraid to play around, at first, with numerous time-frames before you settle on a particular one.

Step 2: Decide on the indicators you will use

Indicators are data points used to help traders spot trading trends and provide them with essential information with which to optimize a trade approach. These data points tie in closely with the time-frame a trader chooses for a trade. There are a number of indicators you can use; one of the more widely used is moving averages. Others include Momentum Oscillators, Bollinger Band and RSI. Once again, your trading style will determine which indicators you decide on.

Step 3: Include indicators that verify trends

There is a phenomenon in the Forex market termed "False trends". This trend is based on false signals that provide an inaccurate representation of economic reality. Various market factors may create a false trend, some of these are timing lags, anomalies in data sources and algorithms. Having indicators to verify or affirm a trend is useful in protecting your trade from unsuspected loss.

Step 4: Decide on how much you are prepared to lose

Considering and defining an amount you are willing to risk on a trade is an important step that many traders overlook. Trading is a two-way street and you can as easily make money as you can lose it. The benefit of deciding on a particular amount is that you can exit a trade as soon as you see the market is not moving in your favor and you lose only that specified amount and not all of your capital. Your risk management technique is an influential factor in how successful you are as a trader.

Step 5: Determine entry and exit points

The entry and exit points you choose to trade with contribute to the profitability of your trade. In determining these points, you will refer to the information provided by the indicator you have chosen for your strategy. If the indicators point to favorable market conditions you may take this as a good signal to enter. Exit points can be decided on various factors. An example of a simple exit point strategy is deciding on a set target. Once the currency exchange price meets that target, you exit the trade. Another exit point technique is to select various factors that will indicate it is time to close a trade.

Step 6: Set out strategy rules

Creating your own trading strategy is not about breaking rules but sticking to them. As part of your step-by-step guide to creating your very own exclusive strategy is taking the time to set out and WRITE DOWN rules for yourself. One of the main determinants of a successful trader is discipline. Unless you stick to the rules you cannot expect your system to generate a profit for you.

No system will ever work for you if you don't stick to the rules, so remember to be disciplined.

Step 7: Test, test, test

Once you have worked out the workings of your strategy, it is time to test it to find out how well it works or to fine tune it and address the kinks. Testing your strategy can be done through a charting software product – one of the quicker ways to test strategy viability. A second method is to practice on a demo account. Honesty about wins and losses is critically important.

How long you test your strategy is up to you, but you should realistically give back testing two months. If you maintain good results consistently for a period of time (once again this is up to you) you can then take the next leap forward and go live. Just remember to take a deep breath first.

The role of Forex indicator in enhancing trading strategy

Forex indicators are especially useful data points that point to the direction or trend in which a particular currency will proceed. Traders use these indicators to gain insight into the market and to improve the profitability of the trading strategies they wish to implement. Indicators can be used in conjunction with any trading style, strategy or time-frame. The trick with Forex indicators is to select the right complement that affirms each other for accurate strategy development. The indicators traders choose must choose the right combination that will help them in profiteering in a fast-moving, fast-changing market.

Different types of indicators

There are a number of different types of indicators that may make choosing the right ones a challenge. Generally, there are two main branches of Forex indicators:

Leading technical indicators

Indicators under this grouping point to possible market movement based on the route a specific currency pair takes or ultimate position a currency pair would attain.

Lagging technical indicators

Indicators under these grouping assist traders in being updated on the latest market movements. Traders use information from these data points to ascertain whether market trends proceeds in a sideways direction or up or down.

7 Important Forex indicators to consider are:

1. Simple Moving Averages

Simple Moving Averages points to the average currency rate for a specified duration (10 minutes, 30 minutes or a day). Each time frame carries the same weight.

2. Exponential Moving Average

The averages, under this indictor, are determined using latest Forex rates that hold a higher weighting in the total average. Traders use this indicator to gain a more precise indication of the market trend direction.

3. Relative Strength Index

This indicator works with a range between 0-100. In using the RSI traders try to spot a point of deviation at which a rate reaches a new high without the RSI exceeding an earlier high. This point of deviation may indicate an imminent reversal. The RSI is widely used by day traders to measure currency price's gains and losses.

4. Moving Average Convergence/Divergence (MACD)

The MACD indicator is based on the charting of two momentum lines. The MACD line is the distinction between two exponential moving averages and the signal line.

5. Stochastic Oscillator

This indicator points to short-term exaggerated buying and selling conditions ranging on a scale of 0%-100%. The Stochastic Oscillator takes into account in the event of uptrend closing rates for specified durations are more intense in the top half of the period's range. The opposite is true for a downward trend where closing rates are focused in the lower half of the range.

6. Bollinger Bands

Bollinger bands are comprised of three lines: the moving average, an upper line, and a lower line. These lines point to the movement of price rate increases and decreases from the averages identified. A price rate that is below the lower line shows potential for a future increase while a price rate that is placed above the upper line, it may indicate a favorable time to sell.

7. Momentum Oscillators

The momentum oscillator indicator is used when a trader wants to establish whether a price rate will increase or decrease. The indicator makes it easy for traders to spot imminent market movement. If the currency rate attains a landmark high while the oscillator is not at the same level, this may indicate a gradual decrease in demand followed by a drop-in price rate.

The ultimate goal of Forex indicators is to assist traders to gain a better understanding of market activity which will allow them to make informed decisions in regard to the trades they enter and exit. The above indicators are by no means the full complement of indicators used by traders, but they do form a good list with which to formulate winning strategies.

Chapter 5: Forex Brokers

Forex brokers are basically middlemen that initiate trades on your behalf. Currency trading brokers, or retail Forex brokers, act as an intermediary that buys and sells assets for a certain amount of commission. Brokers, in general, can be found in various financial markets, including commodities, derivatives, insurance, equities, and real estate. In the past, brokers would initiate trades over the phone. Clients would call in the stocks they want to buy or sell, and the broker would initiate those transactions on their client's behalf for a percentage-based commission.

But, after the technological advancement, everything including Forex trading has been changed. It has been changed in a good way, and it has become easier to trade Forex. However, in modern times, phones have been replaced by the internet. Now, clients can have access to their accounts and make trades using electronic platforms on their computers or on their smartphones. The trades still have to go through a broker who owns the systems that initiate the trades placed by their customers. So, the role of a Forex broker is still active.

Individual brokers were not really that common in the past as most players in the foreign exchange markets were large corporations, importers, exporters, and financial institutions.With the origin of retail Forex and the rise of retail Forex brokers, almost anyone can now make an account and instantly trade online. This is made possible through retail aggregators such as retail Forex brokers, who consolidate trades, made by individuals, which they then trade in the interdealer market run mostly by financial institutions. This made it possible for smaller and individual investors to get into the game despite the small amounts they were trading compared to large-scale financial institutions and businesses. Retail brokers get their prices in real-time through major banks and through the Electronic Broking Service (EBS) system.

Before the advent of retail foreign exchange brokers, trades that were less than US$1 million dollars were discouraged and relatively not allowed in the market. One way this was restricted was through a high bid-ask price that discouraged such trades. The way modern retail Forex brokers make money is through a fee collected from the bid-ask spread. The difference in the spread is the broker's way of compensation for helping you trade. Most brokers also offer their clients a way to make more money from small investments. This is done through margin accounts, which basically entails the broker lending you money to make larger bets on the Forex market. This effectively multiplies a trader's capital by as much as 5,000 percent in some cases.

Anyway, if you want to trade successfully, it is crucial to find the right broker. In an international market like the Forex market, it is pretty hard to find the ideal broker. And there are many reasons why it is hard to find the right broker. One of the major reasons is competitiveness. Yes, nowadays, it is easy to become a Forex broker, and the rate of scam brokers is high. As beginners, you have to be careful when you are making a decision. You might have certain demands related to the tools, platforms, and currency pairs, so if you don't meet the right broker things can get tough. If you have some understanding of your trading style, you can determine the broker successfully. However, if you have entered the Forex market with zero experience, you wouldn't know it. Hence, I'll share some tips to find the right Forex broker.

I know, at times learning the Forex market can be daunting. You can't ignore the important parts of Forex trading. When we talk about important parts, finding the right Forex broker holds a higher place. So, how can you avoid it? If you have selected the right broker, the trading journey will become much easier. We don't say trading is easy, but brokers help you throughout your Forex journey. You let the broker handle your account, with the trust you set on the broker. Perhaps, your great strategies and techniques will become vain if you don't find a reliable broker. If you don't want to fall into any scams, you must select the right broker. For that, consider the following tips.

Focus on your needs

If you know your needs, selecting a broker becomes simpler. Decide what you are going to do. Are you planning for a full-time trading journey or part-time? Are you interested in bigger or smaller moves? There are many brokers out there, but it can take some time to find the right broker. However, before you select the broker, you must consider the capital amount, account type, and withdrawal and fund deposit methods. As there are many brokers, some brokers' offerings might not align with your requirements. Hence, it is important to consider whether the broker offers what you require.

Consider the broker's offer

Now, this relates to the latter section of the previous point. If you are day trading, you can waste time, meaning no 'dealing desk' involved. When dealing desk is involved, it takes a lot of time and will lead to "re-quotes" requirement. When this happens and when the broker questions whether to proceed or not, the opportunity would have been lost. However, to decide on the right broker, you must check whether regulations are perfect. The broker should be regulated in a well-established system. Also, consider these important factors.

Deposit. There are Forex accounts funded with small amounts, maybe as low as $50. But, once you get the leverage, you gain more buying power which is higher than the deposit amount. This is one of the reasons that naïve traders get attracted to the Forex market. Most brokers provide the standard, micro, and mini accounts with different deposit requirements.

Withdrawal and funding policies. Every broker sets withdrawal and funding policies. Some brokers might allow credit card, PayPal, wire transfer, and ACH payment for funding. However, the broker might charge a fee for some services, so inquire about it before you select him or her.

That being said, you must ensure to select the ones regulated by Canada, U.K., U.S., Japanese, Australian, and New Zealand authorities. Find a broker who's available whenever you are in need. You can check whether the broker is responsive by opening a demo account. While opening the demo account, you can send an email with questions that you intend to ask the broker. If the broker provides answers and reverts fast, you can decide the level of responsiveness. If you are not satisfied with their service, don't select that broker.

Find out about regulatory compliance

It is a must for the Forex brokers in the U.S. to be a part of the National Futures Association (NFA) and the U. S. Commodity Futures Trading Commission (CFTC). Once registered, the Forex broker becomes a Retail Foreign Exchange Dealer and a Futures Commission Merchant.

The self-regulated NFA organization is a worldwide industry in the United States. And, it is strict about rules and services so that integrity is protected. This makes the members, traders, and investors adhere to regulatory responsibilities.

The independent government CFTC agency regulates the options and commodity futures in the United States. This agency focuses on protecting the market participants from facing fraud and abusive practices in the financial markets. And they work hard to provide financially reliable markets for the market participants.

However, you must not assume that brokers who own fancy websites belong to NFA or are regulated by CFTC. Instead, you can check whether the membership number of NFA and CFTC regulation is mentioned in the "about us" page of the website. Even countries outside the U.S. will have their regulatory body. So, make sure to consider regulatory compliance.

Look for credible reviews

Written reviews are crucial when selecting the right broker. You might have to read the reviews and check some discussion forums.

However, you can't rely on some random review sites and discussion forums because fake reviews are common. And you'll find both positive and negative fake reviews to make it look reliable. Hence, you have to be really careful when you are looking for reviews. Many naïve traders lose money just because of their carelessness in finding credible reviews. Be mindful of objectivity and get connected with professional traders to get ideas and references.

Don't accept bonuses

When you create a live account, you'll be offered bonuses, but don't accept them. For example, you may receive a $50 bonus for an account worth $500, but it is not going to benefit you because it may link with the withdrawals. Eventually, some of your money will be with the broker. However, when you are creating the account, make sure to send an email mentioning that you don't accept bonuses along with your application. This may help you stay in the safe zone.

Think about the trading platform

Another important factor that is linked with Forex brokers is a Forex trading platform. It is the portal to connect with the market. When you are selecting the trading platform, it is important to consider visually pleasing, easy to use, and a comfortable platform. You must be able to enter and exit trades easily. Also, the trading platform must include a wide range of fundamental and technical tools. If you don't find a broker that offers a well-designed platform, you will not be able to see the trading options clearly. Most naïve traders end up falling for the poorly designed platform, so it is important to do proper research before you settle for a broker.

When you are selecting a Forex broker, you must not be mindless or careless. Instead, you have to be vigilant to select the right broker. Of course, it might take some time, but it is worth it. Only if you have a good broker can you trade successfully!

Chapter 6: Volatility in Forex Trading

In forex trading, the term volatility refers to the degree of risk or uncertainty that occurs with the size of changes in the exchange rate. High volatility indicates that the price of any one currency has changed drastically over a short timeframe. A higher volatility rate indicates that the exchange rate can be spread out exponentially over a huge range of values. On the other hand, lower volatility indicates that the rate of exchange does not change too drastically over a short period of time.

To sum it all up, the high volatility rate means that the trading of the affected currency pair is risky. The low volatility rate, meanwhile, indicates that there are fewer risks in the trade. In most cases, traders use the term volatility to refer to the change in the value of a pair in terms of standard deviation. Volatility is used to quantify the risk of a currency pair over a period of time. Generally, volatility is expressed in terms of years, and it can be in the form of a percentage, fraction or absolute number. In other words, volatility indicates the degree of unpredictable changes in a particular currency pair over time; thereby, it represents the extent of risk that a trader is facing while trading in a particular pair.

Volatility for Market Players

Although many people view volatility as a bad aspect because it represents a negative side of the trade that is; the uncertainty and risk, some traders look at it as a plus for making profits. Market players can find volatility in the market very attractive because it also indicates the possibility of making profits. The chances of reaping massive profits on account of volatility are very high, especially for day traders. However, volatility may not work well for long term traders who prefer to buy and hold.

It is important to note that volatility does not indicate the direction of the market. It, however, indicates the level of moves (fluctuations) of an exchange rate. A currency that has high volatility indicates that there are high chances of an increase or a decrease. A currency that has lower volatility indicates lower chances of an increase or a decrease. One example of low volatility is a savings account whereby the investor does not have chances of losing 50 percent of the money, but neither does he have chances of getting a 50 percent profit.

There is no one currency that stays in high volatility or low volatility forever; there are some time frames when the price of a currency rises and falls so quickly (highly volatile) while other times they seem to be stagnant (less volatile).

There are two general types of volatility, namely historical volatility and expected volatility. Historical volatility is calculated on the basis of past prices while the expected volatility is based on the current prices with the assumption that these prices indicate the expected risks of the asset. One can define Historical volatility as statistical volatility, and it measures the price fluctuations over a particular time. Expected volatility identifies the balance between demand and supply of a currency and uses this to determine the future.

Traders regard volatility as one of the most crucial pieces of information that indicate if the trader should enter or exit a currency position. There are different indicators used to appraise the volatility, and they include Commodity Chanel Index, Bollinger Bands, and Average True Range. All the indicators are comprehensively integrated into most of the trading platforms. The Relative Volatility Index is also another important indicator that reflects the direction that the price volatility is following. The main characteristic of the Relative Volatility Index is that it confirms the RSI, MACD, Stochastic and other Forex oscillators' signals without being repetitive. The Relative Volatility Index serves as a very helpful verification tool because it is drawn from the dynamics of data in the market that are left out by other indicators. When used as a strainer for independent variables, the Relative Volatility index can define the strength of the market trend while measuring up the volatility rather than price.

Foreign exchange traders have for a long time chosen the currency pairs they want to invest in based on the classical analysis of risk and return. Again, the risks and returns are assessed in separate moments and in the best-case scenario, for a certain time series. In real trade, the prices of the currencies constantly change and at different speeds that is, sometimes quickly and other times slowly. As such, a trader should pay a lot of attention to volatility because it measures the price range of currencies in the past, the present and the future comprehensively. Consequently, a trader is able to estimate the potential return and the expected risk of an investment.

Taking Advantage of Volatility

Besides the fact that the foreign exchange market is the largest and one of the most liquid markets, it is also very volatile. Remember that volatility indicates the rises and falls of prices in the markets. The prices of currencies in the forex market can be highly volatile or less volatile depending on the economic conditions. One of the reasons that traders find the forex trade very attractive is the volatility. It offers traders more chances of making quick and huge profits, but one should remember that it also increases the chances of loss. In other words, it is a double-edged sword.

When one observes the forex market closely, he/she will realize that the core of the market movement is volatility. Although geopolitical tensions, market movements, and other factors are the ultimate movers of the markets, volatility rides on the backs of all other factors.

Remember that volatility is classified into two, Historical and expected/implied. There are a number of things that a trader should do in order to survive the volatile market environment. First, the trader should have the possibility to change his/her leverage with ease. Traders use leverage to make large profits when using limited funds. However, this also increases the chances of making extensive losses. Secondly, a trader should not place all his/her trading capital in a single pair currency because the uncertainty is high in the volatile markets. The outcomes are very uncertain compared to normal markets conditions. Therefore, a trader should diversify. Thirdly, a trader should watch out when there are big changes in the forex market and trade smaller. In cases of big movements, a trader should adjust his/her targeted prices. Fourthly, a trader should have the big picture in mind and also monitor trends in larger timeframes. It is even better if the trader can use several timeframes. Finally, the trader should be patient and stay committed to his/her trading plan. Sometimes trading also means staying out of the market; therefore, if a trader is too unsure of what to do, he/she should stay out of the trader.

Technical Indicators of Volatility

A trader can use several indicators to gauge the volatility of a pair of currencies, and as mentioned earlier, the most used three indicators are Bollinger Bands, Average True Range, and Average Direction

Bollinger Bands

Bollinger band indicator was invented by John Bollinger in the 1980s, and it is used to gauge the volatility of a market and to spot the times when prices are about to reverse. They are based on a moving average and normally take into account a 20-period timeframe plotted on a graph. The bands are then formed with standard deviations (two curves plotted above and below the moving average). The theory states that if the deviation of prices indicates a normal distribution, then 95 percent of the fluctuations should fall between the two standard deviations (between the two bands). Any fluctuations that fall outside the standard deviation bands should indicate increased volatility and prices are likely to fall back to their average.

Average True Range

The average true Range indicates the average trading range for a particular period of time. A trading range is defined as that time when a currency trades between consistent low and high prices for a certain timeframe. In a trading range, the upper trading range provides price resistance while that at the bottom typically provides the support. In the case of forex trade, the predetermined amount of time is a 14 period. When the Average true range decreases, it indicates a decrease in volatility. The vice versa is true.

Average Directional Index

The average Directional Index indicates the length of each trend based on the lows and the highs over a particular timeframe. In forex trade, the time frame is usually 14 periods. The indicator is plotted as one line below the chart, and the values range between 0 and 100. When the line is above the twenty to twenty-five levels, then that indicates that a trend is beginning no matter the direction. When the trend becomes stronger, it indicates that there is increased volatility.

Chapter 7: Forex Analysis

Now that you are through with the basic elements that go into every single trade, it is time to delve further into the different strategies to use to determine the possible movements in the market. You must already be familiar with the different factors and forces that cause currencies to gain and lose value over time. This time we will explore the different analytical strategies to put this knowledge to good use. A lot of traders will take pieces of these strategies to formulate their own personalized approach in analyzing currency movement. What is important to know is that there are no perfect strategies, but some trading strategies do work better than others. It is up to you to determine which of these strategies will work for you and your trading comfort levels. Sometimes, even the best strategy will not work. You must not assume that the Forex market will never be beneficial, instead accept the fact that there will be ups and down when trading Forex.

Introduction to Analysis

Forex analysis can be thought of as being divided into two separate analytical schools of thought; fundamental analysis and technical analysis. Fundamental analysis mainly looks at the overall context of a currency, while technical analysis primarily focuses on raw and historical data. Fundamental analysis focuses on economic, political, and financial factors while a technical report focuses on charts, patterns, and other inherent movements.

Fundamental analysts mostly do not consider technical analysis as an effective way to determine the market's movement as they mainly look at the forces outside of the Forex market. The external factors that are primarily looked at are the different relationships of the countries and businesses that directly affect the exchange rates, which include the complex economics and macroeconomics of the factors that drive prices up and down. In contrast, technical analysts don't really pay attention to external forces and are mainly concerned with past rates and data, future trends, and recent patterns. For these types of traders, the Forex market is a self-contained ecosystem with internal factors that determine fluctuations dependent on the buying and selling of different currencies.

As an example, an increase in the value of the euro over the US dollar will be seen by a fundamental analyst as a result of specific changes with the relationship of the EU and the United States. They might also consider factors such as the countries' comparative interest rates and their respective inflations rates. Traders using this school of thought might also try to formulate an educated guess as to whether the trend would continue based on fundamental variables that can be ascertained from sources such as news reports, financial reports, and other predictive data. Technical analysts, on the other hand, will see the rise in the value of the euro to the US dollar as nothing more than a new uptrend. They will analyze both the current and past chart values and using various technical tools, analyze whether the trend will continue or return.

School of Thought Comparison

A lot of new traders would often ask the question, "Which is better?" Technical analysis and fundamental analysis both have their own advantages and disadvantages. The main reason for the divide is primarily because both types of analysis have proven track records of being somewhat accurate. Those who personally prefer fundamental analysis would argue that it has a superior efficacy because the movement in relation to economic data is observable. The connection between economics and the value of their respective currencies is undeniable, while in some cases the relationship may only become clear in hindsight. However, there are some cases where economic strife or improvements contradict market movements in very counterintuitive ways. In most cases, the underlying fundamental factors directly relate to significant currency movements. Traders that quickly jump on these movements, either by their own analysis or through someone else's conclusions, will tend to be greatly rewarded for their efforts.

Meanwhile, technical analysts argue that their method is much safer given that each trade is more specific and has the backing of large amounts of data. Trades using this particular method are every exact, and almost no emotional factor is at play. The types of patterns and data used in this method are quantifiable and observable, negating the need for speculation and argument. Unlike fundamental analysis, which might be up for debate or is subjective, raw data and chart patterns are more exact and concrete in technical analysis. Trades made through this method are only executed when all indicators are supportive of the final analysis.

The ace in the hole for technical analysts in the entire argument is the fact that technical analysis can be applied in almost all types of asset trading, including the stock market and securities market. Fundamental analysts would have to overhaul their previous trains of thought in these markets as they would have to learn its unique framework when compared to the Forex market. Technical analysts will have no problems jumping into these other types of markets given that the charts and patterns still work in the same way. A technical analyst that was previously trading commodities will have no problems jumping into the Forex market; although he or she would have to familiarize himself or herself with the peculiarities of the Forex market beforehand.

Fundamental Analysis

As previously mentioned, fundamental analysis will deal mostly with the external factors that affect the price of any particular currency. Certain factors are quantifiable, while others are qualitative. Some of the more concrete factors will involve economic and financial factors; this includes quarterly earnings reports and economy-related political movements. The more qualitative factors will involve developments in the realm of investor sentiments, political crisis, and other geopolitical developments. Fundamental analysis is sometimes referred to by traders as a complicated art form to master, as it will require a lot of investigative and analytical skills to piece together different factors that will ultimately result in a robust forecast. There are a lot of competing narratives that will often confuse fundamental analysts, but those that can read into the situation will more often than not come up with the best forecasts.

Global Interest Rates and Inflation

Global interest rates play a significant part in the movements within the Forex market. It can also be said that global interest rates rule the Forex market. A specific currency's interest rate determines its perceived value as much as its actual value compared to other currencies. Fundamental analysts closely track and look at each country's central bank and its respective monetary policies. Each country has its own central bank. The United States has the Federal Reserve, the UK has the Bank of England, Switzerland has the Swiss National Bank, the EU has the European Central Bank, and Australia has the Reserve Bank of Australia, and so on.

The main determining factor for the rise and fall of interest rates in any given country is to maintain price stability and control inflation. Inflation is the increase in the prices of goods and services within a country. The sustained increase is closely related to the purchasing power of a country's currency. Hence, inflation is inevitable and is part of a growing economy. A country's central bank will need to control its country's inflation through the adjustment of its currency's interest rate. Too much inflation will directly harm the economy as a whole, and central banks will have to find a way to keep it at a comfortable level to sustain an acceptable growth rate. An increase in interest rates will lower overall growth, while at the same time slow down the country's inflation rate. This happens because businesses will now borrow less money, which will, in turn, prevent their establishments from growing. In contrast, when interest rates are lowered, more businesses will borrow money, boosting expansion, capital spending, and economic growth.

A currency's interest rate will determine how much capital will be going in and out of a certain country. Investors are more inclined to place their money in countries with higher interest rates, thus increasing the demand for that country's currency. The higher the demand, the stronger a currency becomes when compared to other currencies. This also works inversely; when a country's interest rate is low, demand for its currency decreases. This makes that country's currency weaker when compared to other currencies. Fundamental analysts consider these interest rates when trading different currency pairs.

In most cases, interest rates don't change a lot, and changes don't happen very often. Interest rates also don't make drastic movements, which means that if a currency's interest rates have dropped significantly over a long period, it will likely increase again at some point. The key here is to try to determine the direction of the interest rates of a particular currency.

One way of determining the direction of a particular pair's movement using interest rates is through a technique called "interest rate differential." This method typically involves the comparison between one currency's interest rate to the interest rate of its paired currency. The difference between the interest rates is what fundamental analysts look at to determine possible shifts in the prices of the currency. When the interest rates of two currencies move in opposite directions, a significant movement is likely going to happen. That's pretty much about Global Interest Rates and Inflation.

Economic Indicators

Economic factors calculate the statistical information of the country's economy. The economic indicators preview the patterns, performance, and future predictions of an economy. As beginners, you must understand that economic indicators have a massive impact on trading. If you don't understand economic indicators, trading might become complicated. The leading factors of financial systems links with economic indicators. Each indicator differs as per the target group, origin, and on various markets. The indicators are divided by region so that it's convenient to handle and understand, so such divisions are European indicators, Asian indicators, and US indicators. Economic indicators and surveys are often released. However, due to the advancement of technology, anyone can access economic data and indicators whenever they want. As Forex traders, you must understand the impact created by economic indicators on the Forex market. You must analyze them to make a proper decision in trading. So, more important indicators that you must know include:

Interest rates

Unemployment rate

Changes in the Gross Domestic Product (GDP)

Consumer Price Index (Inflation)

Employee Cost Index (ECI)

Purchasing Managers Index (PMI)

Producer Price Index (PPI)

Federal funds rate

Income

Beige Book

Balance of Trade

Mutual Fund Flows

Corporate Profits

Business Outlook Survey

Currency Strength

Consumer Credit Report

Wholesale Trade Report

Durable Goods Report

Employment Situation Report

Industrial Production

Money Supply

Productivity Report

Retail Sales Report

However, you must understand that frequencies of indicators will differ monthly, weekly, or even daily. Only after proper speculation, economic indicators are updated, and Forex and other traders make sure to be up-to-date with speculations. All their trading moves will be based on speculations. When you look at an economic situation, it will have an impact when announced and during the speculation. Both situations will create a shift in the Forex market. For example, when a government issues building permits, there will be more jobs, when there are more jobs, the unemployment rate will reduce. Hence, the consumption rate will increase while resulting in strengthening the value of local currency. Let me put it simply, and an economic indicator will provide the information that a trader needs when understanding the things happening in the economy. If you consider the U.S. economy, it is a happening economy. You will not be able to predict that easily; hence, economic indicators are important to get a good understanding of the market. However, you will come across lagging indicators as well as coincident indicators.

Different traders use economic indicators in different ways. However, to benefit from economic indicators, you must focus on market analysis. You can do primary research or consider analyses, and the choice is yours. For example, when a trader is aware of the event to be taken place, he or she will speculate the market. Based on it, the trader will select a certain instrument to Forex trade. The trader must anticipate the trade properly if he or she wants to acquire substantial profit. When you are speculating the economic indicators, it is important to know about financial events, markets, and all the general factors that will have an impact on the economic indicators. If you are through with these details, your speculation will be firm.

As a beginner, you must become comfortable with using the economic calendar and learn how it links to economic indicators. Once you understand it, you'll get a clear view of its impact on Forex trading. If you utilize economic indicators successfully, you'll be able to achieve success in Forex trading, and you'll learn to manage your expectations as well.

Anyway, before you utilize economic indicators, you must use the information accordingly to match with the context. Of course, raw data is valuable, but you must be vigilant to use it. Luckily, you are benefitted from the profit groups and different governments because they conduct surveys to provide information to the traders. On the other hand, if you try to do it on your own, you won't be able to do it as successfully as profit groups and different governments.

If you want to trade Forex successfully, you must have an economic calendar with the updated information. If you have the economic calendar, it is easy to include all the essential releases and events that will impact the Forex market. For beginners, an economic calendar is one of the most useful tools because it helps to identify the market moves. You can use the forecasted and the actual values to make proper decisions in trading.

You can select a few indicators and master it so that you'll be able to use it successfully when making a trading decision. But, it doesn't mean you can't use all the indicators in trading. Anyway, the choice is in your hand as per your understanding. But remember, you will never find that magic indicator that tells you to trade because there isn't any. It is you who has to use the indicators carefully to benefit from trading.

Debt

Forex debt is something that is unnecessary because naïve traders fall into debts deliberately. Most naïve traders assume high leverage will bring them higher profits. But, when you handle with high leverage even without prior experience, you are pushing yourself to a dangerous situation. Hence, before you begin live trading, you must use a demo account to become familiar with the market. It's apparent that a higher percentage of novice traders lose money because they ignore the logical factors. They are aware that trading a live account without experience will lead to debts, yet they are greedy to make money.

If you think Forex is simple so that you can make easy money, you've got it wrong. Most naïve traders end up facing huge financial losses because they don't have the capital to cover up their losses. However, the underlying problem with Forex debt is greed and improper risk management. If the trader is greedy, he or she may even try to benefit from the last pip. But, one can avoid greed by expanding their vision about market opportunities. And the next is improper risk management, so for this, you must learn the risk management concept before you begin live trading. Even a professional trader must understand risk management to protect the Forex account.

But, if you are already in debt, you must try to save some money to increase your capital. Of course, it will take some time, but you can do it!

Politics

Most beginners don't understand the Forex market. Even though they know about fluctuations in the currency value, they do not know how the currency value has fluctuated. Many factors including politics affect price fluctuation, and naïve traders don't spend the time to understand this overwhelming process. If a country is facing a war, it will have a huge impact on the country's currency value. Basically, political factors may affect a country's currency value positively or negatively. The effect will be based on the war situation of the country. Yet, currency exchange will have some differences. As beginners, you must keep an eye on this! But, remember, stable countries gain more recognition than the countries that don't prevail in peace. Likewise, numerous political factors impact the Forex market. Hence, as traders, you have to keep your eyes open to the changes.

Psychology

Psychology is a huge part of Forex trading. Most professional traders emphasize the importance of psychology in trading. Some professionals believe it is more important than academic knowledge. When we consider the trading mistakes, the basement for the highest number of mistakes would be psychology. Traders are humans, so no wonder that psychology is taking a toll on humans. The constant mistakes are directly related to the psychology of traders.

Different emotions act as a barrier to naïve traders. For example, fear is one of the emotions that constantly attack naïve traders. Even if the trader is confident in trading, it will be hard to make up the mind to enter into trade and the reason is fear. In this case, the trader will be wasting a lot of time trading the demo account. Hence, fear has a huge impact on trading. Of course, human minds look for the safer option, but in trading, you have to handle risks to reach the top. If you are pulling yourself away from entering into a trade, it means you're pulling yourself from the chances of earning profits.

No matter what others say, you will not be able to avoid the trading fear unless you try to avoid it on your own. For that, you must make an effort to understand the trading psychology in detail. But, let me tell you. If you know your weakness, it is more than enough to become successful. If you know that you fear entering new trades, you can work on it and improve your trading behaviors. But, think about the ones who don't know what's going wrong in their trading style. Of course, they will keep on trading until they blow their account completely. Hence, if you know your weakness, you will overcome soon!

Charts

Initially, reading the charts can be confusing, but over time you'll understand. There are different displays as per the price displayed. The Japanese candlesticks are the most common price method considered by most traders. However, candlestick charts are preferred on the Forex chart because it is easier to read. When you are reading the charts, you must use the patterns to understand the price and the market movement. If you don't prefer this, you can opt for line charts. You can find the closing price when you use the line chart. Or you can opt for a bar chart which is just like the candlestick chart. When you make use of the bar chart, you will be able to find the price opened and closed in the Forex market.

The best thing is you can use the technical analysis to read Forex charts. Even if you don't prefer technical analysis, you can benefit from it when you are using it on Forex charts. You can include technical analysis of your charting system because it is allowed by most systems. Yet, try to get the best out of the technical analysis when you have difficulties in identifying the price. Anyway, you must remember that keeping things simple is the best way to trade successfully.

So, there we end Forex analysis. But remember, learning Forex is a continued journey so the more you learn, the more you find!

Chapter 8: Easy Ways to Reduce Your Risks

Trading in the Forex market can be risky. There are a lot of different options to choose from since the market is open 24-hours a day, and you have to worry not only about the two currencies that you want to trade in but also about other countries that interact with your chosen countries. All of this can mean a lot of risk on your part. The good news is that there are some easy things that you can do to ensure that you reduce your risks and see great results in the end.

Research the Economies You Want to Invest In

Research is so important when it comes to picking out the right currency pairs. Not only do you need to worry about the two currencies that you want to work with, but you also have to worry about any countries that trade with those countries, and how changes in that country will affect your trade. The economies of the world can be intertwined a bit and trying to learn what will happen with each one when other events can be a challenge.

You should never just jump into a trade when you join the Forex market. Steady research, including before, during, and after the trade, can make a big difference in the results that you see. Pick out the newspapers, magazines, and other resources that you want to use and then read through them on a regular basis. And always make sure that at least one of your sources gives you daily news so you can keep up with what is happening around you and if any big events will change the value of your currency pair.

Keep the Emotions At Home

Emotions are going to be a deal breaker with any investment. As soon as you allow the emotions to come into the game, things are going to head downhill for you. These emotions can get in the way of clear thinking and often cause you to lose a lot of extra money in the Forex market. Learning how to keep the emotions out of your trades is critical if you would like to make a profit in the process.

This is why it's so important to have a solid trading plan from the beginning. That way, when you enter the market, you know exactly what you will invest in, how long you plan to invest, what needs to happen for you to leave the market, and more. And as long as you stick with that plan, you should be able to limit any potential losses and even help yourself make more money in the Forex market overall.

If you are someone who often falls prey to their emotions, then it may be best to consider a different form of trading. Emotions will force you into revenge trading, staying in the market for too long, speculation, and other behaviors that are risky and can make you lose a lot of money. Sticking with a good trading plan and trading strategy can make the difference in how successful you are with this market though.

Work with a Broker

As a beginner, it is a good idea to work with a broker. The Forex market can be confusing sometimes and having a professional by your side, someone who can answer any of your questions and who will walk you through some of the steps can be a game saver. Add in that brokers often have the platforms that you need, at least the good and secure ones, and it makes sense that you would want to work with a good broker.

Before you pick a broker though, make sure to discuss their fees and any other information with them. Some brokers charge based on how much you trade in the market, and some will charge a flat fee. You will also be charged more or less depending on how much help you need from the broker in the process. Have a listing of all the fees ahead of time so you know how much of your profits will go to someone else.

Put Your Stop Losses in Place

Always make sure that you have your stop losses in place when you begin to trade. These will ensure that you keep your losses to a minimum and help you to keep any of your profits as well. These stop points tell the market when you want to exit, even if you are asleep and can't watch your computer all the time. The stop losses can do a great job of keeping you in the game, limiting your losses, and preventing more risk than is necessary.

First, you must step a stop loss for losing money. This needs to be placed at the point where you are comfortable losing that much money. When the market goes down and reaches that point, your trade will be closed, and you will just have to settle that loss. Even if the market continues to go down, your stop loss took you out and ensured you didn't lose more money.

If you had gotten into the market without the stop loss, you might have wanted to stay in the market and hoped that things got better. Or the downturn may have happened while you were asleep, and you wouldn't be able to fix the issue. Either way, this stop loss can help save you a bunch of money.

You should also put in a stop loss for your profits as well. This will be at the place where you are most comfortable with the profits that you make. Doing this ensures that if the stock reaches that certain point, you will be able to walk away with a profit. This way, if you are away from the computer for some reason, and the currency hits your profit point, but then takes a sharp turn down, you get to take the profit because the system took you out before the downturn occurred. This helps you to maintain your profits and can do wonders for keeping your emotions out of the game.

Never Revenge Trade

Revenge trading can take all of your hard work and throws it down the drain. With revenge trading, the investor often loses money in a trade, and it is usually a significant amount. After losing that money, they panic and decide to try to earn it all back as quickly as possible. They make a succession of bad trading decisions, don't stick with their trading plan, and run into a lot more trouble. Since the investor is not really taking care of their money or the way that they spend it, they end up losing more money in the long run.

Never fall prey to revenge trading. Even after losing money, which is something that everyone runs into at some point or another, just restart and do your trading just like normal. If you find this too hard to accomplish because you got emotionally tied into a trade, this is fine. Just make sure you stop trading for at least a few days and take a break. Once you have regrouped and feel a bit better, and know that you can make good decisions, you can come back and trade the market again.

Find a Mentor to Work With

This can be your broker or someone else you trust and who has spent some time investing in the past. You may find that working with someone who has direct experience in the Forex market is the best but working with someone who has invested at all can make a big difference. This person is perfect to ask questions of, to test out strategies with, and to get some help when things seem tough with your trades.

Most people will be happy to help you with your trades. Just remember to be respectful of the time they are giving you. You may want to bring along some questions and concerns to the meeting and use those to keep the flow of the conversation going. This ensures that you get all of your questions done, without taking up too much time from the individual who agreed to be your mentor.

Of course, you are the trader in this market, and it is your money that is on the line. While your mentor is going to give you some good advice (if you pick the right mentor), you also have to think through the process ahead of time and make sure that any advice makes sense for what you want to do. If you feel that another trade would work better, or you are not comfortable taking that much risk, even if it is recommended by a good mentor, then you don't have to do it.

A good trader can think critically for themselves, and while they appreciate the advice and help, they get from others, it is still important to think through things on your own and consider whether they make sense for your investment or not.

Take a Break When Needed

It can be hard sometimes, but you need to know when it's time to take a break from trading. If you are making a series of bad trades in the market, if you happen to lose a lot of money on one trade, or you just can't seem to get really good results at all, then it may be time to take a break and try again after a few weeks or so have passed.

The problem with staying in the market during these situations is that your thinking is going to become clouded in many cases. The more that you lose, the more that you struggle, the harder it will be to make the decisions that are needed for trading. Taking a few weeks off to clear the head and then coming back fresh can be one of the best decisions that you can make.

Do Not Invest with More Than You Can Afford To Lose

Many traders fall into the trap of investing more than they can really afford to lose. This can be really tempting for those who want to use leverage to make their positions a bit stronger. Unless you have been in the market for some time, it is not a good idea to trade on leverage. This is just asking for the market to go the opposite way of your prediction and can make you lose out on a lot of money in the process.

It is always risky to invest more money than you can afford to lose. Often, the investor will make rash decisions or will decide not to do the right research, and this can result in a disaster. It is much better to figure out how much you can comfortably lose, in case the position is wrong, and then only invest that much. It may limit the amount of profit that you can earn, but it ensures that you aren't left without options and scrounging for the money at the end.

While there is always going to be a little bit of risk when it comes to trading on the Forex market, there are some ways that you can help to reduce the risk and ensure that you see some great results. This chapter provided you with a few tips that will make a difference when it comes to how risky, and how successful, your trade can be.

Chapter 9: Simple Swing Trading Strategies for Forex

Swing trading is a trading style preferred by many retail traders because firstly, they contain entry and exit strategies that do not require one to keep checking the charts every few minutes or hours and secondly, it is a long-term strategy. The trading style is well suited for people with busy lives or even full-time jobs, therefore, cannot afford to watch the charts every other minute.

Traders that use the swing trading technique may use timeframes on the charts from as low as 5 minutes to an hour. Swing traders may combine both the fundamental and technical analysis to draw conclusions and make decisions. To a certain extent, it does not matter whether the market has a long-term trend and/or that the market is range bound because the forex swing trader will not hold the positions long enough for these factors to count.

However, volatility makes significant differences for swing traders because highly volatile markets suit them best. The higher the volatility, the higher the number of movements in the short term. As such, the trader has many opportunities to place his/her trade. Swing trading has a number of benefits including benefits from liquidity, sufficient volatility to create trade opportunities and relatively short time frames to make earnings.

Some traders find the extremely short-term trades exhausting because of the amount of time spent monitoring. They also find long term trading too boring and not active enough with too much demand for patience. As such, they settle for swing trading because it is simpler to use and has friendly time frames. Beginners also prefer this type of trading and try it out with demo accounts before getting into the real business.

In swing trading forex, certain techniques and strategies work well together to get the trader a win. Remember that swing trading is not just a trading style but also a strategy. Within this style, there are different strategies that a trader can use to swing trade safely. Keep in mind that swing trade operates over medium and short timeframes; that is between the day trading which requires a very short timeframe and the positioning trading which requires a very long term. The thing is, swing trading is short enough to create plenty of opportunities for traders but not so short that the trader has to stay glued to the charts. The following strategies are not strictly for swing trading, unlike other technical strategies.

The main concepts behind swing trade strategies are resistance and support. These concepts allow one to choose between two decisions; either follow the trend or go against the trend. The counter-trend strategies seek to make profits when the levels of resistance and support hold up. On the other hand, trend following strategies identify periods where the levels of resistance and support break down. In both cases, it is important that a trader can recognize a price action visually. Remember that markets do not follow a straight line. Even when the markets are trending ultimately, they tend to move in step like movements of up and down. When the market sets a higher high, traders recognize an uptrend, and when the market sets a lower low, then the traders recognize a downtrend. As such, most of the swing trade strategies seek to catch and follow a short-term trend. In other words, a swing trader will be looking for a trend, then he/she will wait for a countertrend, and after the trend has played out, he/she enters the market.

Forex Candlestick Trading

The majority of beginner traders are advised to look for particular candlestick formations that align with resistance and support. This style dictates that one has to be very careful and selective about the trade he/she picks and to stick to the sidelines until everything looks perfect. This style has a chance of making profits, but many people find it hard to make more than just a small margin of profit. There are a number of reasons why people do not make a lot of profit with this style. First, it is very hard to find a set up that looks perfect; therefore, the traders will let many opportunities go. Secondly, the style has very difficult effects on the psychology of the trader because he/she has to sit on the side and watch an otherwise good move get lost.

Consequently, the trader might get itchy fingers in the trade and dive in too deep. Thirdly, when used on its own, candlestick analysis is almost useless. It is used in combination with resistance, support, time of the day, trend and other factors.

All the mentioned factors are more powerful in themselves than the candlesticks, and yet the trader is taught to focus on the candlestick before any other thing. Another weakness of the Candlestick analysis is that it ignores quantitative and fundamental factors.

Trend Trading

Trend trading is identified as one of the simplest and most natural ways or profiting in the retail market. The difficulty with trend trading is that there are a lot of misconceptions surrounding it. This is as a result of the misapplication of analysis methods that are intended for stocks and other commodities. Currency pairs in the forex market tend to move at a lower speed than other commodities and stocks and as such, applying traditional trend breakout strategies without discrimination will result in losses in due time.

Traders who apply swing trading are normally looking to close out the winning trades in one or a few days after the initial transaction. This poses a challenge when one tries to apply a trend trading strategy to the short time frame because the trend trading profits are generated from the big winners after they are allowed to run.

Traders should know that the forex market spends more time in ranging than trending. Even in those cases where the markets are trending, they still range to some extent within the trend with many retracements. Ranging is referred to as "mean-reverting" in technical terms, and this signifies that the prices tend to range back to the average. (Revert to the mean).

Bollinger Band Strategy

The Bollinger band strategy is defined as the continuation trading strategy that uses the technical indicator called 20-period moving average to identify the trend direction. These bands are good for measuring the volatility of the instrument one is trading, and it is used to form a basis of swing trading in the forex market.

The Bollinger bands indicator consists of three lines; lower band, top band, and middle band. When a trader or an analyst is using the Bollinger band settings for the strategy, the three lines represent;

• The Top Line - two standard deviations from the moving average to the upper side

• The Middle Line - is the moving average for 20 periods

• The Lower Line - two standard deviations from the moving average to the downside (middle line)

A trader may try to change the band setting in search or the perfect settings, but there is hardly any such thing. Therefore, anyone who tells you that they are selling the best settings is being dishonest.

The theory behind the Bollinger band is that the two bands (upper and lower) contain price action. This means that any price movements touching or exceeding the upper or lower band indicates increased volatility within the market.

The Trading Rules of Bollinger Bands

Trading the support and resistance of the band lines

A trader can use the upper and lower bands as support and resistance indicators whereby; if the price touches the lower and upper bands and reverses, that indicates the probability of a major move.

Trading the fixed horizontal lines combined with the band lines

In this method, the trader looks for the horizontal resistance and support levels which coincide with the prices that are touching the lower and upper band. The trader should ensure that the price has reversed on this support or resistance level at least once. This makes that trade signal reliable.

Trading the breakout

While trading the breakouts, a trader should watch for the trend process as they break through the lower and upper Bollinger bands. The trader should also ensure that the candlestick is closed above the upper line before entering and that it closes below the lower line before exiting. This technique works best on a trending market.

Trading the squeeze

Firstly, the price must be pushing between the lower and upper bands. Under such circumstances, the market has low volatility. The trader should wait for the breakouts which can either be upwards or downwards. The Bollinger band helps a trader to identify the push and capitalize on the breakout happening afterward. One can place a pending stop order on the two sides' right outside the squeeze. These stop orders will be triggered once the break out happens. When one stop order is activated, the trader may cancel the other one. The trader should then place a stop loss order halfway through the squeeze or on the other side.

Another style of trading with Bollinger band squeeze that a trader can use is to wait for the breakout, once it happens, wait for the price to reverse till it touches the middle band, and then enter the order.

Chapter 10: Simple Day Trading Strategies for Forex that Works

Day trading strategies are very important when one is looking to capitalize on small but frequent price movements. Effective and consistent strategies depend on thorough technical analysis, utilizing indicators, charts, and patterns to anticipate future price movements.

For beginner traders; before anyone can settle in the complex world of extremely technical indicators, he/she should pay attention to the basics of simple day trading strategies. While many people believe that one needs a highly complex strategy to win in intraday trade, straight forward techniques are more effective.

The Basics

A good strategy should incorporate the following factors:

Time management

In day trading, one should not expect to make a fortune if he/she cannot advocate ample time in a day to analyze the charts and new information. The traders must manage their time in a way that they have ample time to monitor the markets and identify the trade opportunities constantly.

Money management

Before the trader ventures into forex markets, he/she should decide the number of funds he/she is willing to risk. While considering this, the traders should remember that the most successful traders will not put more than two percent of the capital at risk in one trade. Either way, the trader has to brace him/herself for some losses if they want to be in when the wins kick off.

Start small

As long as a trader is trying to find his feet in the forex market, he/she should stick to a few stocks preferably 3 per day. It is best if a trader gets really good at a few trades than be average at all the stocks and yet make no money.

Education

In a strategy, the trader should ensure that he/she incorporates education moves. Understanding the intricacies of the market is not all one needs to stay winning, a trader has to stay informed and updated. Any market news and events that might affect the assets should be well analyzed, for example, economic policy shifts. Many resources and materials keep one in the know.

Timing

The forex market gets volatile mostly during the opening hours each day, and experienced traders may be able to analyze the patterns and profits. However, it is advisable that one does not make a move during the first 15 minutes even when the odds appear to be good, the trader should stick to his/her time.

Components that Everyday Trading Strategy Needs

Whether a trader uses automated, beginner or advanced strategies and tactics, three essential components must be accounted for; liquidity, volatility, and volume. Day trading involves making money on tiny movements of prices, therefore, choosing the appropriate stock is very vital.

Liquidity

It enables one to enter and exit the trade quickly at stable and attractive prices.

Volatility

It informs the trader of his/her potential profit range. The higher the volatility, the greater the chances of profit. However, high volatility also increases losses.

Volume

It is the indicator of the number of times an item has been traded within a set timeframe. For the day traders, this volume is referred to as the daily trading volume.

High volumes indicate that there is a significant profit in the asset. Increases in volume normally indicate that a price jump (up or down) is coming fast.

Day Trading Strategies

Scalping

Scalping is one of the most popular strategies of day trading in the forex market. This strategy capitalizes on minute price changes. The power behind scalping is quantity. The traders using this strategy to sell once they identify a profit in the trade. Although this is a fast and exciting strategy of trading, there are a lot of risks involved because of the high trading probability required. The strategy has a low risk-reward ratio; therefore, the trader must have a high trading probability in order to even out. As such the trader should look out for attractive liquidity, volatile instruments and be very hot with timing. One cannot wait on the market, and they need to close a losing position as soon as possible. Scalping strategy is by far the most profitable strategy that one may apply when well mastered, but the adjacent risks prevent it from being the best in the market.

Momentum

Momentum is a crafty trading strategy most popular among the beginner traders. The actions involve acting on sources of news and spotting substantial trend moves that are supported by volume. On a daily basis, there must be at least one stock that will move around 20- 30 percent, therefore, presenting ample opportunities. The trader simply holds his/her position until the moment he/she spots a reversal then closes out.

The other option involves fading the price drop; that is, round the price target immediately the volume starts to diminish. The above strategy is effective and simple when used correctly. However, a trader must ensure that they know the upcoming news and announcements about earnings. A few seconds on the trade makes all the difference to the end of day profits.

Reversal strategy

Reversal trading is used by traders across the world, but it is potentially dangerous and hotly debated when applied by beginner traders. Reversal strategy is also referred to as trend trading mean reversion trading or pull back trending.

Reversal requires the trader to go against the trend, therefore, defy the logic of trading. As such, the trader must be very good at identifying possible pullbacks and also predicting their strength. In order to achieve this, one must have an in-depth understanding and experience of the market.

Pivot points

The pivot point strategy in day trading is very handy for spotting and acting on the crucial support or resistance levels. Range-bound traders can also use this strategy to identify the entry and exit points. Breakout and trend traders can use these points collocate the levels that must break so that a move can be counted as a breakout

How to calculate a pivot point

In forex trade, a pivot point refers to the point of rotation. A trader uses the closing price for trade combined with the high and low of the previous day to get the pivot point. However, it is important to note that if omen uses the price information based on a relatively short timeframe to calculate the points, he/she reduces the accuracy.

The pivot point = (high *low* close)/ 3

With the pivot point, one can easily calculate the support and resistance levels using the following formulas;

First resistance= (2* pivot point) - low

FIRST SUPPORT = (2* pivot point) - high

One can then calculate the second level of resistance and support as follows

Second resistance = pivot point (p) + (first resistance – first support)

Second support = pivot point- first resistance – first support)

Application of pivot point

When a trader is applying the pointy pivot strategy in the forex, he/she will find that in most cases, the trading range for sessions takes place between the first support and resistance levels and the pivot point. The reason behind this is that a high number of traders prefer to play within this range

Traders should also note that this method can be utilized in indexes too. For instance, one can use it to create a viable S&P day trading strategy.

Breakout strategy

The breakout strategy is centered on the times when the price clears a certain level on the chart, with higher volumes. The traders using this strategy enter into long positions once the security breaks above the resistance. They may also do the opposite which is entering a short position when the security breaks below support.

Breakout entry and exit points

The entry points in the breakout strategy are straight forward and nice. The prices set above the resistance level require a trader to take a bearish position while that set below the support level requires a bullish position.

The exit point requires planning. First, a trader should use the recent performance of the asses to identify a reasonable price target. When using a chart pattern, the process will be more accurate. To create a target, a trader can calculate the price swings that occurred recently. A sensible target can include one where the price swing is three points over the past several swings. Once the trader reaches the target, he/she may exit the trade and celebrate the profits.

Limit loses

Day trading is often said to be the swiftest method of making profits in the forex market, but in many cases, the advisers fail to tell the traders that it is probably the most difficult trade strategy that one can master. Consequently, the people who are not well-advised try to trade and fail. In all strategies, the trader should ensure that he/she limits losses especially if they are using margin. The requirements for day traders using margin are usually higher, and when one trades on margin, he/she increases vulnerability in case of sharp movements of prices. Remember that although the margin increases the chances of great profits, it also magnifies losses. In all strategies, the trader should employ stop loss. By nature, Forex strategies are risky because one needs to accumulate profits in a very limited span of time.

Chapter 11: Common Trading Mistakes

Everyone enters the Forex market with the intention of making money. But, not everyone gets to reach the goal of making money. Some traders reach the intermediate level and fail. And some others leave the market right after entering it. But, some traders still persist in trading the Forex market despite the difficulties and risks. What do you think about those traders? Well, the ones who persisted in the market might have had clear intentions of becoming successful in trading. And the ones who failed to remain in the market would have had the thought of making money. But remember, when you set a goal you must have pure intentions in succeeding at it. You must not look at the profits alone. Instead, you must think about success as well.

But there's something I didn't point out above. Yes, trading mistakes. Most naïve traders who leave the market halfway make a lot of trading mistakes. Indeed, Forex is a profit making market, so even a tiny mistake can lead to severe failures. Hence, just like other markets in the financial industry, you must follow a few guidelines to trade Forex successfully. But, unfortunately, beginners don't have the patience to study the guidelines before entering the market. Anyway, I have concluded a list of common trading mistakes made by Forex traders. If you understand the mistakes, you'll be able to avoid making them in the future. As I mentioned earlier, Forex is all about self-learning. So, let's start!

Analysis paralysis

In the Forex market, there are so many opportunities as well as threats. As there are plenty of threats, you must prepare yourself to handle threats successfully. However, most Forex variables distract traders when they are trying to think straight about trading. If you want to find the right strategy, you must overcome all these problems. But, this can be tough for beginners. Anyway, you still have to find a good strategy to trade the market. So, even after finding a good strategy, how can a trader face the analysis-paralysis problem? Yes, it is still possible. Most naïve traders assume that they must look for more because more is considered better. But, in trading, more is never a good thing. Do you think that spending the whole day in front of the screen will help? Well, it will not help. In fact, it will lead to further confusion. You might come across numerous indicators, and it may give the idea that your current decision is false. And, that makes you emotionally weak, so this is when you fall into the problem of analysis-paralysis. The solution is to stay away from the market if you have entered into a trade. The more you watch the market, the more you get confused.

Overtrading

Most beginners don't get to go a long way in trading because they overtrade. This may sound like something simple, but it is not! Trading way too much will lead towards losses. And there is no counter argument on this. The interesting yet sad fact is that naïve traders make great profits in demo accounts, but when they trade live accounts, they trade terribly worse. But, you must understand why this kind of behavior is present in beginners. Basically, when a trader trades the demo account, he or she doesn't become emotional. The reason is that the trader knows the demo account isn't real and even the money is fake. But, remember, if you don't practice, you will not trade well in a live account. The underlying reason for overtrading is emotion. The traders get attached to the market emotionally, and they overtrade as if they will not end up blowing their account. You can actually control overtrading. But for that, you must have a defined plan that you adhere to. To be said simply, instead of trading you are gambling! Instead of trading like a reckless gambler, you must develop a calm and realistic approach to trade the market. Of course, if you have been overtrading for some time, it will be difficult to stop at once. But, for now, you must not trade the live account, instead consider demo trading. Take some time to understand overtrading and the effects of it. Once you understand, you will not make a mistake again.

Risk and money management

Another mistake made by Forex traders is not managing risk and money when trading the market. If you want to achieve success in trading, risk management is important. The simple definition of risk management is controlling the risk to the level that you can handle. The beginners often follow this denial concept. They deny the fact that they may lose any trade at any time. They believe all the ads and fabricated stories about quick money in trading. Hence, they don't give enough attention to risk and money management. Just think, how reasonable it is to risk more than the amount that you can handle losing? Sounds insane, right? But, this is one of the most common mistakes. A single trade can wipe your account completely if you don't control the risk. If you don't manage risks, you are going to lose everything. If you are dreaming about profits, it is a good sign because you are motivated to make profits. But, if you are dreaming ONLY about profits, then it is not a good sign. You must think about losses as well. You must find the risk ratio that you can afford to lose. Most professional traders and Forex mentors recommend 2% risk, but still, the decision is in your hand. You must decide the ratio that you are comfortable with.

Improper or no trading plan

Not having a plan or having an improper plan both fall into the same category. Having an improper plan is more like having no plan. So there is not much difference. This is also another mistake made by naïve traders. Most naïve traders assume that they can create a plan later but that later never comes. Besides, you must have a plan when you enter the Forex market because, without a plan, it is tough to enter into or exit a trade. A plan makes you stick to your goals. When you don't have a plan, you tend to make decisions emotionally. You will pick some random trading strategy, and you will use any approach to enter into a trade. Plus, you will exit a trade without considering any important factor. Thus, if you have a plan, you'll plan your trade execution. Before selecting a trading strategy, you'll shortlist some of the strategies. And you'll have an exit plan. Likewise, you'll be trading like a professional. Of course, even professionals must have a plan. But more than a professional, a naïve trader must have a plan to keep things organized. It is crucial to have a written plan that acts like a roadmap. Honestly, there are numerous benefits that you gain from trading with a plan. If you don't believe it, you can test it on a demo account. Typically, when you do something without a plan, your vision will be absurd. Thus, a plan keeps your vision clear. You will know when to exit a losing trade and when to extend a profitable trade. So, it is all about having an effective trading plan!

Trading or gambling

Trading and gambling are two different things. But, due to greed, the difference between trading and gambling have become something that is hard to define. Of course, beginners have the urge to enter into the market. But once they enter, they don't think about ethics and morals. Instead, they develop a gambling mindset. They start trading as if they have been practicing trading. Well, you must not enter the live trading account if you have not mastered your trading strategy, techniques, or approaches. The way to differentiate yourself from a gambler is to practice trading. You must start with a demo account. Remember, you must not trade the demo account for the sake of trading. Instead, you must trade it for a certain period until you become comfortable with Forex trading. But then, some traders will not have real emotions when trading the demo account. Hence, it can be tough to manage emotions while trading the demo account. So for this, you must try your best to keep your emotions real while trading the demo account. Only if you keep your emotions real will you be able to manage to live trade successfully.

Ignoring stop-loss

There can be times when you are confident about the profit targets. But, it is always better to focus on stop-loss placement. You already know that Forex is a volatile market where things can change in seconds. There can be certain events that will change the currency values in a short time. These events will have a huge impact on your trading decision. Hence, stop-loss will protect your account from facing losses. Thus, even if you are a professional trader, you must not ignore stop-loss placement.

Avoiding news releases

You must understand that news releases have a huge impact on the Forex market. Certain economic factors will create changes in the currency pairs. Thus, even if you are not a news trader, you must keep an eye on the news releases because it will affect the currency value. If you avoid news releases, you might make huge mistakes, so it is better to keep yourself updated about the news releases.

Increasing trading positions

Some naïve traders are overconfident, so they believe that their trading targets 100% profitable. So, even if their anticipation doesn't go in the right direction, they still believe that the trade is going in the right direction. And they simply add more positions with the hope of a price reversal. If you make this mistake, you'll be increasing the losses created. If it's an open position, you must never add more positions to it because it will become a chaotic situation. So, don't add more positions to trade if you are not experienced enough to understand it.

Currency correlations

Forex traders believe that they can earn more profits if they take more than one day trade. Of course, you can make good money, but on the other hand, losses will be doubled. When you trade multiple trades, you will also be dealing with currency correlation. When the currency correlations have a similar setup, both losses and profits can occur. If you are handling with currency correlation, you must remember that you are dealing with risks.

Revenge is not sweet

If you are a naïve trader, losses can be tough for you. But that doesn't mean professional traders are happy about losses. Even the professional traders don't prefer earning losses, but they don't take revenge from the market. On the other hand, naïve traders take revenge. The revenge trading will not do any good to you because you will end up facing losses. However, to avoid all these you must accept the fact that losses are possible in trading. You can't run away from losses. But, you can always limit losses. Hence, instead of revenging the market you can focus on improving your trading style.

Lack of knowledge

Actually, I should have added this mistake to the top of the list. When you don't have the Forex knowledge, you are likely to move towards losses and failures. To enter into profitable trades, you must keep improving your trading skills. If you aim to become a skilled trader, you must keep feeding Forex knowledge. Try to learn new trading techniques, methods, approaches, blogs, and educational books about Forex trading. You must only enter the Forex market after understanding the whole market. Most naïve traders don't make an effort to learn the market, so they lack the Forex knowledge. If you are assuming that trading strategy will help you to support trading, you've got it wrong!

Along with the trading strategy, you must have all the other important knowledge to trade Forex successfully. But remember, the knowledge that is not practiced is worthless. Hence, you must practice demo trading with the knowledge that you have acquired through learning.

Improper trading goals

I know, money is important. But if you begin your trading journey with the ONLY aim of making money, it will be the same reason why your journey will end. If you want to become a profitable trader, you must set proper trading goals. If you stop aiming for money alone, you will be able to improve your trading path as well as the account. When you run after money without thinking about anything else, you might break Forex rules and trade without a limit. Maybe you might earn a few good trades initially, but in the long run, you will not be able to create a successful trading path.

Selecting the wrong broker

Most naïve traders don't select the right broker because their complete attention is on making money. They don't think about the ways to make money. Only if you find a good Forex broker will you be able to manage your trading account successfully. Also, your success begins when you find a good trader and deposit your capital on the trading account. If your account isn't managed successfully, you will end up losing your money. Hence, you must allocate time to find the right broker. You can use the tips that I have mentioned already.

Not knowing the purpose

For some naïve traders, Forex trading is an entertainment. They find out about Forex trading in an ad, and they think it will fun to trade Forex. So they just enter into the Forex market. But, this is not the purpose of Forex trading. If you are entering the Forex market, it is important to know for what purpose you are entering the market. Your purpose will decide your level of commitment, attitude, and the goal. Thus, set your purpose wisely to make money from trading. You must be consistent in trading if you want to see yourself as a successful trader.

Being greedy

The beginners are usually greedy to make more money in trading. In fact, greed is the main factor that makes traders fall into traps. Most beginners enter the Forex market with the wrong intention, and they assume they can become rich quickly. When you become greedy, you will begin to chase unrealistic goals. Of course, you can set goals, but it should be realistic. Only if you set the right goals, you'll be able to overcome mistakes. So for that, you must avoid being greedy to make more money.

Not understanding Forex psychology

You must understand that Forex psychology has a lot to do with Forex trading. In fact, it is one of the major parts of trading. Some traders fail to trade the Forex market successfully because they don't understand Forex psychology. Most Forex mistakes can be avoided if traders understand Forex psychology. But, naïve traders don't even consider Forex psychology as a part of the trading journey.

It is not easy to learn the mistakes and to correct them when you are trading Forex. But, you are lucky because you are warned about the mistake beforehand. So when you are trading, you'll not make most of these mistakes. Studying and learning the market will always be beneficial so you don't have to think that learning the mistakes is a waste of time. Let me tell you, even if you learn these mistakes over and over, you will still make certain mistakes. But, remember to correct them to become a noteworthy trader.

Chapter 12: How To Succeed In Forex Trading

Finally, we reach the last part of our A-Z forex learning journey. But, you must not limit learning here. Forex education never ends because you have a lot to learn. For example, when you are trading you will come across a new strategy, so you must allocate time to learn it. Likewise, maybe some professional traders will find a new trading technique to trade Forex, so if you happen to find details about that technique, you must learn about it. Likewise, education will tag along with you when you are trading the Forex market.

As a beginner, you must understand that the Forex market often changes, so as traders you must pace along with the market changes if you want to make the right trading decision. Also, the Forex market has both pros and cons so as traders you must know about it as well. If you are looking for some proven secrets to trade Forex, there isn't any. The way to trade Forex is complete in the hands of the traders. To trade Forex like a pro, you must be mindful and skilled! Plus, if you don't understand the importance of learning, you will not be able to begin trading. Like already said, self-learning is the key to successful trading. If you want to learn Forex, you have plenty of sources online. In a digital world like this, finding learning sources is not a big deal.

As a beginner, you will find it hard to focus on learning without directly trading the market. But, once you start learning, you will feel good about learning the market without directly trading because you need to know how to trade the Forex market. When you learn, you must put them into practice on a demo account. As it is free of charge, you don't have to worry about using it for too many times. Even through demo trading, you will be able to analyze your performances. But, for that, you must trade the demo account without considering it as a demo account. You must look at it as if it is your live trading account. Once you do follow this technique, you'll be able to apply everything that you learn on a demo account and test. Plus, this practice session will be effective as you are considering the demo account like the live account.

Basically, Forex is accessible, educational, and profitable. Of course, no trader can accuse that there are no opportunities because there are plenty of opportunities. Like for everything else in this world, even the Forex market has negative factors. One of the negative factors is risks. Yes, the market is highly risky, so naïve traders tend to fail as soon as they enter into the market. But, risks in the Forex market is not the only reason for their failure, rather their negligence too. Nowadays, naïve traders don't enter the market with a proper goal. They aim to make millions overnight which is impossible because Forex isn't a casino. In the beginning, the learning procedures may seem difficult, but over time, you will understand, and you will get through the process of learning the Forex market. Also, remember, if you learn Forex successfully you will be able to trade successfully.

Before you enter the Forex market, you must set goals that you can achieve. Don't try to set goals that are absurd, for example, becoming rich in a month. Of course, some traders set such goals because they have not understood the market properly. Anyway, quantifiable goals will take you a long way in trading. The goal that you set must be simple to understand and value. You must also focus on the goals that can be attained in the long run. It is much better to set monthly, weekly, and yearly goals so that you will stay on track throughout your Forex trading journey.

Once you have determined the goal, you must then focus on the methods to achieve it. For example, you can consider the capital amount, the amount you are willing to risk, the trading strategy that you are going to use, and much more. If you have a proper idea on what you are going to do, you can then create a defined trading plan. Your plan should have everything including the trading strategy that you are going to utilize in trading. Also, don't forget to have your trading journal. So with that, you can enter into the Forex market and trade. But that's not all, let me share some tips to succeed in your Forex trading journey.

Don't ignore the money management concept

If a trader wants to succeed in trading, this is one of the concepts he or she should never ignore. Through hedging or Stops, your account will be protected from facing a loss. Hence, you must use the Stops when it is necessary. If you don't want to face losses and if you don't want to blow your account, you must make sure to focus on the risk-reward ratio, stop-losses, and many other factors that relate to the money management concept. Even if you select the best trading strategy, you will not be able to make a profit if you don't utilize risk and money management concepts perfectly.

If you want to trade, just start

Most newcomers have the habit of delaying, and maybe it is because they are afraid of the market. But, for how long can they shy away from the market? Hence, you must understand one thing, if you can do something today, just do it. To become successful, you must do it today because procrastination is not safe. If you have learned to trade, now it is time to trade the demo account, so don't delay it, do it today! Success begins today, right now!

Keep practicing

Some people say it is better to keep practicing, even if we are good at it because it will sharpen the skill even better. Similarly, in trading, you must have the demo account throughout your trading journey. Even if you become a professional, you might need it when you find some new strategies. However, as a beginner, you must keep practicing until you are confident to trade the live account. As you have the demo account, you don't have to worry about anything.

Know your trading limit

As a naïve trader, you must never try to invest a huge amount in a trade because you don't have the experience in trading the market. Hence, try to begin small when you are starting your trading journey on the live account. It is not a must to invest a huge amount if you want to make a profit, because even a smaller investment will return a profit. When you begin small, you will have less risk to handle. It is better to begin trading without involving many risks so that you can control your emotions.

Focus on single currency pair

This is an unpredictable market, so some traders find it complicated. To become a successful trader, you might have to do a lot of things. However, one of the most important thing that you must do is to trade a single currency pair. You can find the pairs that you are comfortable with so that you will not have to face trading issues. When selecting the currency pairs, try to select the ones that are mostly traded, so it is easy for you.

Let the risk rate remain the same

When you gain a few good trades, you may feel as if you can now increase the rate. But, don't do it. Of course, when you succeed your level of confidence increases, but you must not make quick decisions. In fact, most traders have lost just because of this confidence. Hence, you must not increase the risk rate just because of a few successful trades. You must remember this tip if you want to succeed in trading.

Maintain patience

Most naïve traders lose their patience when trading. But, it is reasonable because they are losing their hard-earned money. But then again, the Forex market doesn't force you to trade the live account. Instead, it offers the demo account. Hence, it is your mistake if you are directly trading the live account. And some other traders want to trade the market every day, but do you think it is practical? Will it benefit? Can you earn a profit if you trade daily? Well, you must have the patience to wait until there is a profitable signal because, if not, you might end up overtrading. Definitely, through patience, you can trade Forex successfully.

Be consistent

This is one of the important factors that you must remember. Before you begin live trading, you must have some understanding of the trade execution. You must have a trading method. It is important to gather the information needed to make a proper decision. You can use fundamental or technical analyses, but what matters is consistency. You must be consistent in trading with the trading method that you have selected.

Become discipline

If a trader is not disciplined, it is impossible to expect other things like a trading plan, trading journal, and many other factors. Only through discipline, all these factors shape up. The beginners will have difficulties in maintaining trade discipline because they don't have experience. So for that, the beginners must spend a day analyzing and watching the charts without entering into any trades. Even if the trader witnesses a highly profitable trade, he or she shouldn't enter into it. You must be able to remain calm. You must be a disciplined individual if you want to become a disciplined trader. Only a disciplined trader can become a professional trader.

Appreciate yourself

You might be trading a few profitable trades, and there can be some losses as well. But you must not worry about the losses made because losses are unavoidable in Forex trading. Instead, you must allocate time to understand the reasons for the losses. And then, as you have made some profitable trades you have the right to celebrate, so treat yourself for the profits. Make sure to note down the trading strategy and techniques used in those trades as well.

Don't try harder.

Usually, professional traders will not try harder to find the right trade that they should enter into. If you can understand the market and if you can read the charts, the profit signals will be visible when you look at the charts. You have to try hard to find the right trading opportunity, but you should never try harder because when you try harder, you don't find the right trading signals. Instead, you somehow convince your mind to accept a certain trade signal as profitable. And then, if you enter into that trade by accepting that trade signal, you will not be making a profit most probably. Hence, it is better to try, but you shouldn't try harder when you are in the Forex market.

Don't do it for the money

You must not trade for the money, then, for what else should you trade? Actually, you must not use the Forex market today to settle your payments tomorrow. Meaning, you must not solely rely on the Forex trading income until you become a well-versed trader. Also, you should not quit your day job until you master trading successfully. However, most naïve traders don't listen to this advice and end up without both trading and their day job. Hence, it is not something recommended. You must, of course, trade for money, but don't treat it like the main income until you become a professional trader.

So, there we go with a list of things to do to succeed in Forex trading. Remember, Forex trading is related to the way you think and the way you handle. Your thoughts must be clear, and your mindset must be stable if you want to become a successful trader in the Forex market. Therefore, make sure to keep yourself up-to-date with Forex knowledge.

Chapter 13: Best Tools and Software

For centuries now, traders have used Forex Tools to increase productivity through improved performance. Ever since the early times of human existence, people have evolved and learned how to use tools to make their life easier. Imagine that some years back, people would not easily communicate with each other and currently, people are communicating with each other as soon as they want regardless of the time and the distance.

Tools are literally indispensable in life especially in the current years, and this case also applies for forex trading too. Brokers make a point of providing traders with some of the most advanced trading platforms to help them get the best experience and maximize profits. One example of this is Meta4, but many tools are more powerful and other features that enhance the trading experience. Without trading tools, Foreign exchange can be very challenging for both the new and seasoned traders. As such, many traders look to complement their decision-making skills through the use of different trading tools. The tools help the trader determine the most profitable exit and entry point.

Forex tools are provided by the brokers and platform providers for free, or the user may be required to subscribe for some. Some of the free tools offered by most websites dealing with forex and financial news are the economic calendars. Some forex signal trading services also provide the traders with trading cues that help the beginner traders.

Some popular online trading platforms such as Meta Trader 4 offer a compilation of the best trading tools. In particular, Meta Trader 4 offers a cover −all package of trade indicators and trade automation options.

Fundamental analysis tools are some of the popular and most useful tools of the trade that a trader can get online for free. Some of these tools include the economic news calendar and financial newswire access. Other tools of trade available for the trader can be found on different platforms and forex news.

Economic News Calendar Tool

Economic news calendar is one of the most essential and useful tools of the trade used by traders. The list informs the trader of the future market consensus and also the previously released information about the relevant geopolitical events and key economic data. The calendar also lays out the timings of monetary policymakers' speeches, central bank policy statement, and elections. Fundamental analysts have a special interest in the calendar because of the fundamental economic releases that will affect a country's currency. The typical providers of these calendars include brokers and news websites.

Financial Newswire Access

As a supplement to the calendar, economic news gets disseminated by a range of financial publications. The news outlets include respected newspapers and financial wires such as Reuters, Market Watch, Journal, and the Financial Times. There are also other publications and source online that are less know but viable. These tools analyze the important economic news, geopolitical and geographical events, and other resources such as gold and oil that can affect the urgencies value.

Pip Calculator

A trader may have a hard time working with different currencies expressed as pips especially if they do not understand the pip valuation system. In forex, a pip is the smallest trade unit for every currency pair. The worth of the pip usually differs based on the pair in question (Base currency and secondary currency). A pip calculator helps the trader to determine the value of a pip with regards to their position size in their local currency.

A typical pip calculator may also show the value of a pip for a particular pair based on a mini lot, micro lot, or standard lot. To use the calculator, one simply needs to enter the position details that include the currency pair, the trade size, the amount of money in the account, the position size parameters and the leverage. The calculator works out the value of the pip for each position in the chosen currency. The tool is very useful for the trader to keep track of the value of a position in the account.

The Currency Correlation Tool/Correlation Matrix

The forex market is made up of many pairs of currencies and there exists known correlations that one can easily calculate. The correlations can either be positive or negative, and they will be more pronounced in some currency pairs than in others. Having a negative correlation indicates that the pairs will move in different directions. A positive correlation means that the pairs will move in the same direction. A trader who seeks to diversify will normally opt for the negatively correlated pairs.

Broker Spread Comparison Tool

Many of the spread comparison sites show the spreads that are quoted by the brokers usually on major currency pairs. Majority of the spread comparison websites allow a trader to filter timeframe, session or currency pair, therefore, giving a trader an edge when selecting the broker with most affordable dealing spreads. Once the trader has selected the broker, a spread comparison tool becomes pretty useless because switching the brokers after a selection can be very costly.

Forex Time Zone Converter

The periods when a trader chooses to participate in the market can make a major difference to their gains. The major forex trading centers in the world include London, Tokyo, New York, and Sydney and they all operate in different time zones. However, to some degree, the business hours of these centers overlap with Sydney opening the market on Monday at 5 pm NY time and closing at 5 pm on Friday NY time. One of the most useful tools that a trader can have when trading is a graph that shows the times that the different centers are operating. This is true because a trader will be able to identify the moments when the markets are overlapping, and these are usually the most active and liquid times. Remember that the three most essential ingredients of trading are volatility, liquidity, and activity.

Forex Volatility Calculator

As seen earlier, one of the most essential elements of trading is market volatility. The currency pairs with limited ranges are barely the best currencies for trading. There is no difficulty in calculating the volatility, but with the numerous numbers of pairs available for trade in the market, it is better if the trader allows a properly programmed computer to handle the task. Typically, a forex volatility calculator will determine the volatility of every pair in real time by taking historical exchange rate information. Another aspect of a good forex volatility calculator is that it breaks down the volatility into different timeframes for instance weekly, monthly, quarterly and annually. This helps the trader to determine if an option is too volatile or not.

Forex Trading Platforms

Meta Trader 4 is the most used online trading platform, and so far, no other platform matches it. The platform has a variety of features that are literally indispensable for a serious trader.

This platform offers a wholesome technical analysis functionality which allows traders to map out currencies in real time. It also allows the trader to apply a variety of technical oscillators and other relevant indicators to the currencies. The platform also has a functionality that is fully integrated to allow the trader to trade currencies directly from the charts. An extra advantage of the Metatrader4 is that traders can use it to transact with most of the forex brokers online. Again, a large group of people use the platform; therefore, if one runs into problems when using it, he/she can ask for help. Meta Trader 4 also supports expert advisor software and automated trading.

Meta Trader 4 also allows the trader to add their own parameters in the premade and custom indicators. Besides the stock exchange, MT4 allows traders to deal in other asset classes such as energy products, metals, and stocks so long as they are supported by an online broker.

Doubtlessly, MetaTrader4 is by far one of the best, useful and complete forex trading tools in the market and it is obtainable for free from the website of the developer. Always open a demo account and practice before investing with real money.

Keeping a Trading Journal

One might underestimate the importance of keeping a journal that records the history of different trades. An accurate journal is one of the most essential tools that helps a trader determine their next move. It is important to keep track of the details of each trade, for instance, the time a trade was initiated, why, and if it was liquidated, what the driver was. The trader will be able to assess his/her trading habits from this information, learn from mistakes, and mitigate risks in the future.

Conclusion

You have been given the best strategy to start trading forex. You still need to do the legwork to determine which currency pairs are actively moving right now and in what direction they are moving.

Please do not use this book as a "magical" investment solution. Yes, you can invest and make money right now. But, it all depends on the amount of research you have conducted to learn the currency pairs, while you read through this book.

You know whether you are a low, medium, or high risk investor. You have to establish your strategy and entry/exit plan based on your risk aversion. If you have a high risk aversion, then you want to trade with low risk of your capital.

You learned that you do not want to invest without looking at:

• The global economic perspective
• Both countries' economic situation
• Technical data to see current trends

As long as you know the big picture, narrow it down to a specific set of currencies, and establish the market trends and potential change in that trend, you can make a profit. It may only be a few dollars or whatever your currency is at first, but it is better to make a small profit over a long period of time than to lose big and try to get it back in a panic.

You have been given suggestions only. You are going to narrow down what works best for you as you get more comfortable with all the information. Once you reach that point, you still need your due diligence and discipline, but you will start to see the profits you have worked hard for.

Nothing comes easy in life. Nothing is magic. You just need to follow the steps outlined in strategy 3 to determine the proper and comfortable entry/exit point for each trade based on the current market conditions.

Don't miss out!

Visit the website below and you can sign up to receive emails whenever Leonardo Turner publishes a new book. There's no charge and no obligation.

https://books2read.com/r/B-A-XCJI-MIUZ

BOOKS 2 READ

Connecting independent readers to independent writers.

Did you love *Forex Trading For Beginners The Ultimate Strategies On How To Profit In Trading And Generate Passive Income*? Then you should read *Stock Market Investing + Real Estate Investing For Beginners 2 Books in 1 Learn The Best Strategies To Generate Passive Income Day Trading, Investing In Stocks, And Investing In Real Estate* by Leonardo Turner!

Stock Market Investing For Beginners:

This guidebook is going to spend some time taking a look at the stock market and how you can get started. We will start out with some information on what the stock market is all about, some of the benefits of choosing this as your vehicle for investing, and even some of the different options that you can choose from when you are ready to invest in this market.

Many people have considered going into the stock market, but they are worried that they won't be able know how to enter the market or they will not find the right strategy that can help them be successful. This guidebook is going to help with this problem because it provides you with some of the best strategies possible, that even a beginner can get started with and see success in no time.

Have you ever heard of technical analysis, fundamental analysis, income investing, the CAN SLIM strategy, or anything else that is similar to this? These are all strategies that can be very useful when it comes to working in the stock market, and all of them can help you get a great return on investment when you get started.

In addition to talking about some of the great strategies that come with the stock market and all the different options that you can work with, you are sure to find a lot of great information, tricks, and tips that will ensure you can see success as a stock market investor. Even beginners can be successful in this endeavor, and this guidebook will give you the tools that you need to make sure that you attain the goal you want.

Whether you are a beginner or a beginner to investing in general, or you have been investing for some time, and you are now interested in starting out with the stock market for the first time, this guidebook will have all the strategies, tips, and tricks that you need.

Real Estate Investing Blueprint For Beginners is going to take some time to explain all of the things that you need to know to get started with your first rental property. We will discuss the importance of financial freedom and how real estate investing, especially with rental properties, will be able to help you to reach those goals of financial freedom.

From there, we are going to dive right into the process of searching for and finding the perfect rental properties for your needs. We will look at how you can look for a property, how to get the right financing, the importance of doing an analysis on the property, and even how to determine your return on investment to determine if you are actually going to be able to earn an income on all of the work that you do.

In the final section, we are going to discuss what you will need to do when you actually own the property. We will look at how to find the right tenants, how to maintain and fix up the home, how to collect rental payments, and even how you may work with a property manager to help you get the income, without having to be there and help your tenants all of the time.

Getting started in rental properties is going to take some time, dedication, and so much more. But for those who are looking for a good way to increase their financial freedom, and who want to be able to own their own time, then this is one of the best investment opportunities for you to go with. When you are ready to get started with your own rental property investment, make sure to check out Real Estate Investing Blueprint For Beginners to help you out!

Also by Leonardo Turner

Real Estate Investing Blueprint For Beginners How To Create Passive Income On Properties To Escape The Rat Race And Reach Financial freedom
Stock Market Investing For Beginners Learn Strategies To Profit In Stock Trading, Day Trading And Generate Passive Income
Stock Market Investing + Real Estate Investing For Beginners 2 Books in 1 Learn The Best Strategies To Generate Passive Income Day Trading, Investing In Stocks, And Investing In Real Estate
Forex Trading For Beginners The Ultimate Strategies On How To Profit In Trading And Generate Passive Income

CPSIA information can be obtained
at www.ICGtesting.com
Printed in the USA
LVHW041419111020
668515LV00002B/487